PRAISE FOR *CIVIL UNITY*

"Shola has a genuine commitment to creating a better world. *Civil Unity: The Radical Path to Transform Our Discourse, Our Lives, and Our World* is the perfect read for anyone who is seeking to not only transform their own life but also to be a catalyst for positive change in the world. It will become your resource for inspiration, guidance, and a road map toward a more harmonious and enlightened future."

—SIMON T. BAILEY
Author, *Resilience@Work: How to Coach Yourself into a Thriving Future*

"You NEED to read this book. It's an incredibly powerful and compelling guide for restoring much-needed kindness to our divided world."

—MEL ROBBINS
New York Times bestselling author
Host, *The Mel Robbins Podcast*

CIVIL UNITY

SHOLA RICHARDS

CIVIL UNITY

The Radical Path to Transform Our **Discourse**, Our **Lives**, and Our **World**

Forbes | Books

Published by Forbes Books, Charleston, South Carolina.
Member of Advantage Media.

Printed in the United States of America.

10 9 8 7 6 5 4 3 2 1

ISBN: 979-8-88750-489-6 (Hardcover)
ISBN: 979-8-88750-490-2 (eBook)

Library of Congress Control Number: 2024907405

Cover and Layout design by David Taylor.

I'm dedicating this book to me. More specifically, I'm dedicating this book to my younger self. To the kid who was constantly scared, confused, and searching desperately for kindness, I'm writing every word of this for you, young Shola. Hopefully, this book will finally give us the healing that we both need.

CONTENTS

INTRODUCTION

The most important decision we make is whether we believe we live in a friendly or hostile universe.

—ALBERT EINSTEIN

"Do you believe that we live in a friendly or a hostile universe, Shola?"

At the end of one of my virtual Zoom presentations, a participant in the session typed the Albert Einstein quote shown above into the chat box, followed by the question directed squarely at me.

Even though the question was challenging, I had an answer for her immediately. But before I get to my response to the question, it is important to note when the question was asked.

It was the summer of 2020. We were three months into a deadly global pandemic that was the source of fear, confusion, anger, and grief for many people. We were five months away from one of the most divisive presidential elections in American history. And, a few short weeks earlier, the brutal murder of George Floyd under the knee of a police officer had broken open the world unlike very few things before it.

Personally speaking, during that time, I was falling in and out of my own personal depression. My keynote speaking and consulting business that I worked tirelessly to build two years prior was on the verge of collapse (being dependent on gathering large groups of humans together in the same room is *not* the ideal way to make a living during a global pandemic). The exhaustion of simultaneously trying to rebuild my business and parent my two daughters—who were ten and seven years old at the time—while trying to pull off a bootleg version of homeschool for them almost destroyed my sanity and theirs. Not to mention, whenever I foolishly attempted to escape to the television or to social media for a break, I was greeted with the aforementioned George Floyd murder on endless loop, unceasing political melodrama, friends and colleagues who surprisingly revealed themselves as racists, rising COVID-19 death counts, and a nonstop stream of evidence that our world was more divided and uncivil than ever before. I felt trapped, incompetent, sad, alone, terrified, and defeated on a near-daily basis.

Yes, that all sounds horribly depressing (because it certainly was at the time), but context matters, and I wanted to ensure that you knew my state of mind when that question was asked to me. My answer to the question in the Zoom chat box was simple and quick: "Einstein was wrong."

The Real Decision

I'm aware that nothing screams delusions of grandeur more than implying that you know better than one of the greatest minds in the world's history, but what I felt in that moment four years ago is what I feel as I'm typing these words now.

The most important decision we make isn't whether we believe that we live in a friendly or hostile universe. If that were the case, then I don't know anyone on that day in 2020 (or today, for that matter) who believed that we lived in a friendly universe. The evidence to the contrary was so overwhelming that if the universe were on trial for hostility, the guilty verdict would be locked in before the jury's DoorDash order arrived at the courthouse.

That's why I'm not on board with the idea that deciding whether the world is friendly or hostile is the most important decision we can make right now. Once we make the decision that Einstein mentioned, then what? In my travels, I've encountered countless people all over the earth who have decided that the world is not simply "hostile," but it's an irredeemable dumpster fire as well. The common solutions that I've seen after making that decision are to complain about it to anyone who will listen, watch hours of cable news each day to reinforce how right they are about their stance, or fall into a fog of helplessness—none of which is particularly important or helpful.

The real decision is if we will actively create a universe that is friendly or hostile.

I know that sounds like I'm playing semantically with Mr. Einstein's quote, but I promise that's not the case. Decisions have the luxury of staying safely in our minds, away from the action that will give those decisions life. Sure, some decisions can inspire us to take action but not always—and that's my concern. Even worse—in some cases, our decisions can delude us into believing that we've acted, when in reality, all we're doing is talking and thinking about action. Simply put, deciding if we believe that we live in a friendly or hostile universe will not be nearly enough to meaningfully transform our discourse, our lives, and our world.

Action, on the other hand, means that we are doing something more than making this an intellectual exercise. We're taking the hard step of pulling something from our minds and bringing ideas into the world where it can benefit us and others. In terms of our social discourse, many people have firmly decided that our current and common way of interacting with one another is unacceptable, but how many people are *actively creating* a kinder and more civil world through their words, actions, and behaviors?

I don't have an exact number, but I can confidently say that it's not enough. But how are we supposed to create a kinder world while sharing it with mean-spirited, hateful, and potentially dangerous people who want to do us harm? That's what I want to address in this book.

First things first, though. This book is about action. It is not an understatement that I am obsessed with the need for us to become active participants in rescuing our discourse from the abyss. The common perception is that collective faith in the goodness of humanity is fading fast, and as more people choose to close their hearts and turn inward—or close their fists and swing them outward—the less chance there will be to create a friendlier universe. The only way to reverse this disturbing trend is to take uncommon action to fight for our shared humanity.

I think that I know exactly how to do this.

Transforming Our Discourse, Our Lives, and Our World

When it comes to honoring our shared humanity and transforming our discourse, our lives, and our world, there is one word that comes to mind: "civility."

More specifically, we need to actively engage as many people as possible around the restorative power of civility, and we need to begin now. The willingness to unite our world by modeling civility—and encouraging others to do the same—is not only a courageous act, but it's also an unusual one in these divisive times. I am calling this radical act "Civil Unity," and I believe that it has the power to change everything.

To ensure that we are unifying behind the same idea, I define civility as the active demonstration of respect toward others and the ability to disagree without disrespect.

When I've asked my clients all over the globe why they are losing faith in the goodness of humanity, their answer is always the same: *we don't respect one another.* And as previously mentioned, the evidence is overwhelming.

The best among us—teachers, healthcare professionals, grocery store employees, election poll workers, flight attendants, and public servants—are being viciously harassed, and in some cases physically assaulted, for simply doing their jobs.

Depraved social media trends that glorify bullying, violence, and hate are on the rise (if you can stomach it, type the "George Floyd challenge" into Google to see what was trending shortly after his murder in 2020).

Workplaces continue to cowardly turn a blind eye to toxic behaviors that are literally reducing the life span of their employees.

Bad faith actors who traffic in misinformation and disinformation are deepening our divisions, contaminating our discourse, and reducing the faith in the goodness of our fellow humans.

Political divisiveness that's off the charts.

Racism, anti-Semitism, Islamophobia, homophobia, and misogyny.

That's just the everyday stuff. That doesn't include the more extreme situations like the multiple wars raging abroad, mass shootings in our communities, and crimes against humanity occurring throughout the world on a near-daily basis.

Everything that I just mentioned are examples of how a lack of respect for our fellow humans is making the world a more hostile place, and I wouldn't blame you for feeling helpless when you read this. But you're not helpless. You have agency to do something meaningful to turn this around, but first I need to check the state of your heart and mind. When you think of the current state of the world, are you good with this being the price of admission for living at this time? If you're a parent, is this the world that you want your children to inherit? Assuming that the answer to both questions is a resounding, "Hell no," you are ready to engage in the heavy lifting that's ahead to heal our world.

The lack of civility toward others is the primary reason why people believe that we live in a hostile universe. So dear reader, let me ask you this:

What are you going to do about it?

No need to look around—I'm not asking the collective "you." I'm asking *you*. If you don't know how to answer that question, the good news is that I'm writing this book to ensure that you have a clear answer to this persistent problem.

Why I'm Writing This Book and the Hard Questions about Civility

My sincerest hope is that the book you're about to read will become the definitive guide on how to restore civility to our discourse. That isn't hyperbole my friend; I'm dead serious about this.

To be clear though, this is not about the "Civility 101" silliness that will barely move the needle. If you're looking for tips on how to smile bigger, have happier thoughts, and turn the other cheek when faced with cruel behavior that's harming you and others, then we should kindly part ways now. I'm going to tackle the upper-level curricula in this book. Incivility is a formidable force that has defeated countless challengers who have stood in opposition to it, and we must bestow our fullest respect before engaging it in battle. Toothy grins, toxic positivity, and cringey team-building exercises that a sleep-deprived squirrel could devise won't come close to slaying this beast.

To ensure that you are aware of what we're dealing with, here are some of the most commonly asked questions about civility that I have received from all over the world:

How can civil discourse be maintained during disagreements about topics that are profoundly polarizing, such as abortion, gun control, or politics?

How can I be expected to be civil toward someone who has deeply wounded me—the drunk driver who killed my child, the relative who sexually assaulted me, the spouse who left me for my best friend, or the narcissistic parent who abused me? More importantly, why in the hell should I be civil to them?

How can I be civil when confronted with the hatefulness of intolerances such as racism, misogyny, anti-Semitism, homophobia, or Islamophobia?

How can I have a civil conversation with someone who isn't tethered to reality? Do you know how hard it is to respect someone who believes in baseless dark web conspiracy theories?

It sounds like civility means that we just need to be agreeable, not rock the boat, avoid having opinions or keeping them to ourselves, and not taking a firm stand against the policies and people who are trying to harm me and my loved ones. What in the world is positive about any of that foolishness?

Tough questions, right? Believe it or not, these are only a sampling of what I'm hoping to address in the following pages. As mentioned, unifying our world around the power of civility is a radical act, and it's not for the faint of heart. The challenges ahead require some very creative solutions, and we must be fully prepared for the labor that is ahead of us.

While true, I still haven't told you the real reason why I'm writing this book.

OK, The Real Reason Why I'm Writing This Book

Yes, I do want this book to be the definitive guide to bring civility back to the world, but there's more to it than that.

Nearly twenty years ago, I attempted to end my life, in large part because of the incessant incivility that was beating me down on a daily basis. It was one of the darkest periods of my life, and it never gets easier to discuss this publicly or privately.

I'm what many people refer to as a highly sensitive person or an empath. All of my life, I have felt things very deeply, and while this trait has numerous benefits, lately it just feels like a curse. I feel like the rudeness, incivility, and lack of kindness and respect in the world are slowly killing me. During the past couple of years, I have been more terrified than ever that those demons that tormented me into a suicide attempt two decades ago will revisit me again.

Before you dismiss me as a thin-skinned snowflake unable to navigate the harsh challenges of the modern world, please know that I'm not alone in feeling this way. We are currently in a mental health crisis, and the lack of civility is contributing to it in a major way.

During my speaking engagements—and, despite the fact that it kills a piece of my soul every time—I share the story about my suicide attempt from the stage. Like clockwork, within minutes of exiting the stage, I'm met by a line of people who fall into one of three categories: (1) they have a loved one who has died by suicide, (2) they have attempted suicide, or (3) they are strongly considering suicide based on how mean-spirited the world is today. It is beyond heartbreaking.

I'm writing this book to help them—and yes—to help me.

If you give a damn about creating the friendly universe that Einstein was talking about—and I'm assuming that's the case, because you picked up a book called *Civil Unity*—then we cannot allow this to continue. We're on the fast track to kill ourselves and destroy the planet if we do not wake up to this reality and start taking different actions.

I want to live in a friendlier world, but I'm tired, y'all. I'm tired of getting on flights and seeing passengers berate the flight attendants. I'm tired of going to my young daughters' sporting events and seeing out-of-control parents cursing out the referees (who, as a reminder, are mostly volunteers!) as if it's Game Seven of the NBA Finals. I'm tired of our elected officials being more interested in scoring cheap political points against "the other side" with a fifteen-second sound bite on social media instead of legislating like the mature adults they promised us they would be. I'm tired of hearing about the families who dread the holidays, the employees who hate going to work, and the people who are crippled with anxiety because they do not know how to disagree without disrespect.

In other words, I don't want to live like this anymore, and as mentioned, I'm not alone.

Maybe the problem isn't incivility, but instead, it's a lack of understanding about the action we must take to create the friendly universe that Einstein was talking about. One thing is for sure—you will know exactly what to do to create a friendlier universe after reading the following pages.

I've waited my entire life to write this book, and I couldn't be happier that it's in your hands now.

My apologies to Mr. Einstein, but we're way past deciding if we are living in a friendly or hostile universe. It's now time to unite around the goal of actively creating a friendlier and safer—and quite frankly, *better*—world for all of us.

If you're up to the challenge of making this happen, let's begin.

PART 1

THE FOUNDATION

CHAPTER 1

What Is Civility, and Why Should We Care?

Don't be a hard rock when you really are a gem.

—LAURYN HILL

I wish that I had a cool origin story like when Peter Parker was bitten by a radioactive spider and became the iconic Spider-Man.

Unfortunately, the origin of my civility story isn't cool, heroic, or fun. It's actually pretty cringeworthy, and I have actively—and unsuccessfully—tried to forget it for nearly four decades.

I was eleven years old when my dad accepted a professor position at a university in Greensboro, North Carolina, which meant that our family had to move from my beloved hometown of Amherst, Massachusetts. Even though we spent only a year in Greensboro before moving back to Amherst, those 365 days were transformative for me, and that year fundamentally changed how I viewed the world.

One day stood out from the rest.

We were about three weeks into the school year, and my fifth-grade teacher assigned our class a math test, and I remember having to urgently use the restroom. As a painfully shy kid who rarely advocated for his own needs (especially as the new kid in school), it was like an act of Congress for me to respectfully raise my hand and quietly ask if I could take the pass to use the restroom.

I still remember my teacher's undisguised disgust at my question and then her flatly saying, "Sure … once you're done with the test."

Wait, what?! Done with the test? The test was five pages long! I wanted to stand up and yell, "Look, lady, you don't get it. My bladder is about to explode like a Molotov cocktail if I don't relieve myself in the next thirty seconds. Give me the damn restroom pass NOW!"

Yeah, there's no way I'd ever say that.

So instead, I stared helplessly at the pages of unsolved improper fractions that needed to be converted to compound fractions as if they were schoolyard bullies getting ready to kick my ass. At this point, I had only three options: (1) brilliantly solve all of these questions in record time, (2) give up and turn in an empty test and get a grade of zero, or (3) pee in my pants. And as mentioned, I had only thirty seconds to decide before the decision was made for me.

I should mention that in addition to failing to advocate for myself, I was also indecisive. Those two less-than-useful personality traits pretty much set the table for the only predictable outcome of my dilemma: *I peed in my pants while sitting at my desk.* On a positive note, my light brown corduroy pants absorbed most of the pee. The bad news is that the remainder that was not absorbed by my pants formed a yellow puddle under my desk that slowly became noticeable by my classmates.

There are no words that I can conjure on this page to accurately describe how mortifying this was for my fragile eleven-year-old psyche. If it was possible to die from embarrassment, there is no question that the coroner would have placed a toe tag on me and marked the time of death as a puddle of my own urine pooled around my feet while taking a math test.

Once my teacher finally noticed my accident, she gasped in horror and demanded that I go to the restroom (a little too late for that, isn't it?). Unfortunately, that meant that I needed to stand up from my desk in my pee-soaked, light brown corduroys and make a walk of shame that I will never forget as long as I live. The laughter was deafening, the experience was brutal, and, for the first time in my life, I literally—not figuratively—wanted to die.

As I ran to the restroom fighting back tears, for the first time, I asked the question that would shape the course of my life.

Why can't we be kinder to one another?

That was the origin of my civility story. After that fateful day, I asked that same question almost every day for the next twenty years.

Living in Fear

Miraculously, I recovered from what should have been a fatal blow to my fifth-grade social life to make some great friendships while I was in Greensboro. Not to mention, some of the best food that I've ever eaten was enjoyed while I was there (hush puppies, in particular). Overall, despite an extremely rocky start, I loved my time there.

Still though, that year in Greensboro fundamentally changed me. In addition to "pee-gate"—if you have a better name for that catastrophe, I'm open to suggestions—it was in Greensboro where I was called a "nigger" for the first, and sadly not the last, time. As a quiet, polite, and friendly kid, it was very difficult for me to accept the idea that some people would be unkind to me because of something that was out of my control, like the color of the skin I was born in.

To be clear, this wasn't something that was inherently wrong with Greensboro. Looking back on my childhood, I realized that I experienced similar behavior while living in Amherst, too, including one particularly traumatic episode.

One day, shortly before moving to Greensboro, I got off the school bus near my house in Amherst. After exiting the bus, two older boys led me into the nearby woods where they wanted to "show me something cool." I will spare you the details of what happened next, but I will share that I was sexually assaulted by those boys, and it took me decades afterward (with the assistance of therapy) to help me to process that episode and how deeply I repressed it.

One thing that I do remember clearly was the decision that I made as I was forced into an unwanted sex act. I remember, as a young boy, consciously thinking to myself, "If I let them do whatever they want to me, they may appear to like me briefly." At least that's what I told myself in order to get through that encounter and allow me to sleep at night. It was only later when I realized that incident was the source of my bladder control issues, which ranged from wetting the bed multiple times a week to peeing all over the floor in my fifth-grade classroom in Greensboro. I have never discussed this story with anyone outside of therapy, but as a nearly fifty-year-old man, I decided that I finally need to own this story instead of it owning me.

In my formative years though, that story did own me. The realization that there are mean-spirited people in the world who derive a sick sense of joy from hurting other people scared the hell out of me as a young child. As a result, I began to live in fear of these people as I tortured myself with the same question over and over.

Why can't we be kinder to one another?

After two decades of asking that question without receiving a useful response, I realized that I didn't want to live in an unkind world.

So, I decided to leave it.

The Search for Civility, Acceptance, and Death

It's a strange feeling to decide to end your own life.

I can't speak for anyone else with suicidal ideations, but on that autumn morning when I decided definitively that would be the day that I would die by suicide, it didn't feel like a major decision at all. I've spent more time agonizing over how to set my fantasy football lineup for the week than I did deciding if I should live or die. In my mind, I was already dead inside, so it only made sense to get on with the business of making it official.

What was I running from?

What was responsible for killing my soul and leaving me dead inside?

And what specifically was the pain that I desperately wanted to end?

Before I answer those questions, I need to explain a little bit about myself first. It's also why I care so deeply about civility.

As mentioned in the introduction, I'm an empath—which is a fancy way of saying that I feel things very deeply. It may sound lovely to experience the emotions of the world so vividly, and it is, until it's not. When I witness or experience heartless, violent, hateful, and cruel behavior, it eats away at my heart like a flesh-eating virus. This may sound strange, but I literally lose sleep over this stuff. Worse still, I have always held on more deeply to the things that hurt me than the things that brought me joy. I know that I'm not alone in this.

As the desire to end my life metastasized in my brain, I reflected back on a saying that I heard on television shows growing up: *Sticks and stones will break your bones, but names can never hurt you*. I despise that phrase with the fire of ten thousand suns. It hit me with a double whammy of awfulness, because it wasn't true, and I felt a deep shame because I did let the words hurt me. If I knew how to get the words to stop hurting me, I would.

Fast-forward to the morning of my suicide attempt, and all that I could think about was the cartoonishly cruel treatment and mean-spirited words that I was dealing with from my workplace colleagues at the time. And on that fateful morning, I had reached my emotional limit for accepting unkindness. I grabbed my car keys from the hook near my front door and said quietly to myself, "I can't live like this for another thirty years, another thirty days, or even another thirty minutes."

I craved kindness, civility, and respect as much as I craved my next breath. And in the years prior to my suicide attempt, I went to some extreme lengths in hopes of receiving the kindness I desperately craved.

Some of the more egregious examples included having friends who used me as the butt of their racist jokes, and I would force laughter out of my lungs in hopes of convincing them that I found their humor as funny as they did. I sat in silence as my classmates viciously and repeatedly mocked a kid with Down syndrome, because I didn't want them to turn on me if I stood up for him. I let my boss punch me—yes, you read that correctly—because I failed to read her mind, and I immediately slithered on my belly to her office (figuratively speaking) begging for her forgiveness for making her so angry.

I could fill this entire book with examples of the soul-decaying things I did as I chased kindness and respect, but if you are anything like me, who wants to read that? You get the point. In addition, worse than being an empath, I was also a doormat. Worst of all, I concluded that the common denominator in all of these situations was me, which confirmed a belief that I spent my entire life running from: *I must not be worthy of kindness.*

This was the belief that effectively killed my soul.

So, instead of craving the kindness that was constantly eluding me, I started craving something easier and more realistic. Something that I could control. *Death.* Or more specifically, an end to the constant pain of not receiving kindness that my death would provide.

As an empath, I couldn't ever dream of shooting myself in the head, slashing my wrists, or overdosing on pills, because I didn't want to hurt any of my loved ones by finding me in that state. So instead, while driving down the 405 freeway in Los Angeles on the way to my toxic job, I attempted to drive my car off the freeway overpass to make it look like an accident.

For reasons I will never understand, the guardrail on the freeway held firm, and with extreme gratitude, I'm still here. Ever since my suicide attempt, I finally stopped asking myself the question that I first asked while shamefully hiding in my pee-soaked pants in an elementary school bathroom.

Instead, I have been single-mindedly focused on action—specifically, taking action to create a world where kindness and civility are the norm. If I must live in a world where I feel emotions deeply, then I will spend the rest of my life working to alleviate my emotional suffering and the emotional suffering of others.

That is what I believe the radical act of Civil Unity can do.

The Strength in Kindness

Civility is an interesting concept. For my fellow etymology nerds in the house, the root of civility comes from the Latin root *civilis*, which means "befitting a citizen." Needless to say, being hateful, rude, homophobic, or a bully is not befitting of any reasonable citizen.

The beauty of civility is that it's apolitical. It's something that we feel strongly enough about that we will teach it to our children, whether we're Democrat, Republican, Black, white, Latinx, Asian, transgender, cisgender, gay, straight, Jewish, Muslim, Christian, or atheist. Strangely, it's the one thing in our divided world that we collectively agree is important, yet it's the one thing that many of us consistently fail to do.

This failure is costly, because civility is the solution to society's most pressing questions. Do we want less toxicity in our politics? Do we want a safer world to live in? Do we want a world free of hate and discrimination? Do we want to work in organizations that allow us to do our best work? Do we want our children to learn in schools that are kind and supportive? Do we want to live in a world that prioritizes our mental health and overall wellness? If your answer is yes, then steel yourself for the reality that uniting around civility is the only thing that will get us there. Everything meaningful in our world requires civility as its foundation. Yes, everything.

Unfortunately, for us, civility is not something that's enforceable—it's not like I, or anyone else, can make you do it. In that sense, it's like flossing our teeth, exercising regularly, or choosing to stop watching cable news. It's not something that you have to do; it's only something that you should do if you care about maintaining your health. Until civility graduates from being a "should" to a "must," we're going to remain stuck on the sidelines while we watch our discourse continue to circle the drain. That's why I'm screaming from the rooftops that this is a must, and it all starts with kindness.

At the heart of the civility that I'm advocating for is kindness. Many people use the words "kind" and "nice" interchangeably, but they are not the same things. "Nice," by definition, means to be polite and agreeable—and hopefully, we can agree that this is a ridiculously low bar. Some of the meanest and most hateful people on earth can mutter a "please" or "thank you" once in a while.

Being nice certainly has its place, but in terms of meaningfully changing the world, it's a fairly impotent practice. Nice people often avoid necessary behaviors that improve society, such as having difficult conversations, holding people accountable, honoring themselves, or standing up for others for fear of rocking the boat or appearing impolite. Not to mention, niceness is the birthplace of passive-aggressiveness. I'm sure you've encountered a "nice nasty" person like this in your life before: "Good job on the presentation that you delivered this morning. It was way better than the one you delivered last month. We're all so happy to see that you're finally improving. Bless your heart." *Ugh.* We need to drive a few exits past niceness if we're serious about bringing civility to the world.

Prior to my suicide attempt, I was the prototypical nice guy (thankfully, minus the annoying passive-aggressive traits). Afterward, I chose to leave niceness in my prior life and embrace kindness instead. Kindness is about demonstrating through our actions that we sincerely care about another human being. Kindness comes from a place of sincere benevolence, and it is significantly harder than sprinkling niceties around. It is kind to have a challenging conversation. It is kind to tell someone that their actions are harming another person. It is kind to be concerned about problems that don't affect us directly. It is kind to take action to build a better world for everyone. Kindness, unlike niceness, is hard work.

On that note, can we put to bed the idea that kindness is weakness? In our extremely polarized world, kindness is one of the most surefire demonstrations of strength in existence. As humans, we are hardwired to fear people whom we perceive to be different from us. To overcome our evolutionary programming and offer compassion, goodwill, and altruism to others whom we perceive to be different from us is an uncommon act, and it's something that the weakest among us lack the courage and conviction to do consistently.

In summary, nice is something that you do, whereas kind is something that you are. To engage fully in this work, we need to be kind.

So, let's revisit my definition of "civility" that I mentioned in the introduction: the active demonstration of respect toward others and the ability to disagree without disrespect.

To ensure that there's no confusion about it, I will take a deeper dive into the definition's two parts.

The Active Demonstration of Respect toward Others

Respect is the lifeblood of every functional interpersonal relationship, but what if it was the consistent lifeblood of our interpersonal interactions?

Can you imagine a world where we are united on the goal of treating others with dignity, thoughtfulness, consideration, and courtesy, consistently? I can. In fact, I dream of that world every day. That's what respect is, and I believe that we can do this regardless of our perceived differences or personal beliefs. Before continuing, it is important to preemptively address a thought that may have crept into your mind after reading the preceding sentence: *What about people whom I don't respect? Why in the hell should I offer civility to the assholes who are making the world a worse place?* That is a fair point and one that will be unpacked in painstaking detail in this book—I promise.

Before we get there, I want to ensure that we're operating from the same shared language when it comes to respect. Like most things, as my teenage daughters like to say, there are levels to this stuff. On that note, following are the levels of respect. My goal is to keep the barrier to participation extremely low by keeping this excruciatingly simple. Needless complexity will not serve us in this work, and I want as many people as possible to engage in this important effort. This is not meant to be an exhaustive list, so I'm listing only the most critical items. Bear in mind that this is just a start, and you are more than welcome to add anything that you feel is missing.

A word of caution, though—please don't dismiss what you're about to read as common sense. You might not believe this, but I'm typing this sentence on a flight from New York City to New Orleans, and there is a gentleman across the aisle from me who is using his iPhone charging cable to clean between his toes. He is literally flossing the cord between his toes with such vigor that any dental hygienist who witnessed his efforts would slap a gold star on his chest. In what universe is this OK?

Common sense is not that common, my friend.

Level 1 Respect—The Basic Skills

- *Common Courtesy:* Saying "please" when you make a request, "thank you" when someone does something for you, and sincerely saying "I'm sorry" when you make a mistake or hurt someone (intentionally or unintentionally).
- *Being Honest:* Telling the truth, keeping your word, and honoring your commitments and promises.
- *Kindness:* Treating others with compassion, fairness, and dignity.

Level 2 Respect—The Intermediate Skills

- *Being Inclusive:* Accepting and embracing our differences (race, religion, sexual orientation, physical ability, age, country of origin, gender, or socioeconomic status) and acknowledging the value and worth of others.
- *Actively Listening:* Listening attentively to others and being fully present when they are speaking and not swiping through your cell phone or interrupting them.
- *Being Considerate and Self-Aware:* Being aware of how your words and actions affect others and being mindful of others' feelings and of your surroundings (the guy

sitting across from me in Seat 2D hasn't mastered this point yet).

Level 3 Respect—The Advanced Skills

- *Resistance:* The willingness to speak up against incivility, hate, or abuse.
- *Honoring Boundaries:* Respecting others' privacy, personal space, and their stated boundaries.
- *Disagreeing without Disrespect:* The ability to stay respectful despite a difference in opinion.

Each level of respect jumps up in difficulty, and how far you choose to go in your civility practice will determine the level of respect that you will share with the world. As you already know, there is a sizable amount of folks who haven't mastered the basics in Level 1. My challenge to you in this book is to consistently practice these skills until they become second nature. If more people simply did these nine things consistently, the world would become a more civil place, overnight.

Please note that a key part of my civility definition is the word "actively." Yes, it is important to have kind and compassionate thoughts toward others, but if we are not actively demonstrating kindness and compassion, does it really matter what we're thinking? One thing is for sure, though—a more civil world is an impossibility without actively operating from the foundation of respect. It is our actions that are either harming or helping the world, and the more people who are engaged in the latter, the better.

Let's revisit these "respect" behaviors. Think about how you felt when someone failed to do these basic things:

A terse email hits your inbox from a colleague demanding that you do something. You picked up your friend's kid from the airport in the middle of the night, and the kid (or your friend) didn't bother to say thank you. Your neighbor borrowed your lawn mower and broke it and didn't apologize—not to mention, offer to fix or replace it. You're sharing an important update with your boss, and he's too busy swiping through his cell phone to acknowledge anything that you said. You had a scheduled first date with someone whom you really liked, and she stood you up. You let a friend drive your car, and he left it full of fast-food wrappers and ketchup smears on the seats. If you are anything like me, situations like these can cause you to lose faith in the goodness of humanity.

It's possible that you might be thinking, "Hey, that's life! Not everyone is going to care about your precious feelings. People need to toughen up and stop being offended by everything all of the time."

Yes, noted. I'm not saying that the solution to our civility issues is to magically live in a world where thoughtless and rude behavior doesn't exist. If that place existed, I'd already be there happily sipping a mango margarita, reading a book (instead of writing this one), and hanging out with my loved ones in peace. What I am saying is that there is no utility in making excuses for people who consistently treat others poorly. It's like the person who uses the guise of being authentic, keeping it real or being brutally honest as cover for being mean to others. Two things on this: being brutally honest is nothing to be proud of. Have you ever noticed that people who claim to be brutally honest rarely, if ever, share their honest opinions that are uplifting, encouraging, and kind? The world is plenty stocked with brutality, and there's no need for any more of it. Second, and more importantly, if you are driven by the need to defend harmful behavior, please stop.

Sure, it's one thing to acknowledge that not everyone will care about our feelings, but does that mean that we should normalize it when people behave disrespectfully? If your coworker Jason is known for raising his voice at his colleagues, making homophobic jokes, and heating up his homemade fish tacos in the break room microwave, should we just helplessly shrug and say, "Well, that's just Jason being Jason"?

Screw that. It's not normal to show a lack of respect to our fellow humans, and our learned helplessness of allowing it to continue only succeeds in causing us to lose faith in the goodness of humanity and deepen our incivility crisis. We need to stop confusing what's common with what's normal. Worse, it's the normalization of rudeness, thoughtlessness, and selfishness that serves as the foundation for more severe examples of lack of respect like racism, intolerance, and violence.

That's the problem I'm trying to fix in this book.

I know not everyone is going to care about this stuff. There will always be the people out there who weakly accept the disintegration of respect as the way things are or the people who derisively call people who care about creating a more respectful world as "bleeding-heart crybabies"—and that's fine. I'm not writing this book for them. *I'm writing this for you.* The steady slide into incivility will not stop when those folks wake up and start being respectful. It will stop when the rest of us make a collective decision to interrupt this toxic pattern by loudly declaring that this isn't OK and then taking action to do something about it. I'm done waiting for everyone to get on board with this idea. *I just want you to get on board with it.*

It begins with the understanding that an active demonstration of respect is the critical first step in building a civil world. And that's only the first part of this civility formula.

The second part is much harder.

The Ability to Disagree without Disrespect

What happens as a society when we are unable to disagree without disrespect? A lot of things, and unfortunately, none of them are good. In their latest report, *Civility in America VII: The State of Civility*, leading civility researchers Weber Shandwick and Powell Tate, in partnership with KRC Research, shared the top consequences of incivility. Most are borne from a place of being unable, or unwilling, to disagree without respect:

- intimidation and threats
- violent behavior
- online bullying and cyberbullying
- harassment (verbal, physical, or sexual)
- discrimination and unfair treatment of certain groups of people
- less community engagement
- feelings of isolation and loneliness
- less political engagement[1]

Please look at that list again. Can you see how our inability to disagree without disrespect is deeply damaging our world and our way of life? Whether it is in the comment section of a social media video, at a local school board meeting, or in the halls of Capitol Hill, our collective inability or unwillingness to engage in the hard work of disagreeing without disrespect is eroding the fabric of our society.

---

1 Civility in America VII: the State of civility, https://webershandwick.com/uploads/news/files/Civility_in_America_the_State_of_Civility.pdf.

Don't just take my word for it. Let's dive deeper into the research.

- In a survey of two thousand middle-school-aged students by the *Journal of School Violence*, it was found that cyberbullying victims are almost twice as likely to attempt suicide than non-victims.[2]
- According to Pew Research, the percentage of U.S. adults receiving physical threats online has doubled since 2014.[3]
- One in three women globally (that's approximately 736 million women) are subjected to physical or sexual violence by an intimate partner or non-partner (a number that has remained unchanged for the past decade).[4]
- According to *The State of Workplace Discrimination 2021 Report*, 55 percent of people surveyed have experienced discrimination at their current company, 61 percent have witnessed discrimination at some point, and only 54 percent who reported have had their matter fully resolved.[5]
- More than one in three adults aged forty-five and older feel lonely in the United States.[6]

Before you drop this book to run to the nearest bakery and eat half of your body weight in muffins, please know that I'm not trying to depress you.

---

2 Josh Howarth, "17 Cyberbullying facts & statistics (2024)," November 22, 2023, https://explodingtopics.com/blog/cyberbullying-stats.

3 Ibid.

4 Carla Drysdale, "Devastatingly pervasive: 1 in 3 women globally experience violence," March 9, 2021, https://www.who.int/news/item/09-03-2021-devastatingly-pervasive-1-in-3-women-globally-experience-violence.

5 AllVoices Team, "The state of workplace discrimination 2021," December 14, 2021, https://www.allvoices.co/blog/state-of-workplace-discrimination.

6 Centers of Disease Control and Prevention, "Health risks of social isolation and loneliness," https://www.cdc.gov/emotional-wellbeing/social-connectedness/loneliness.htm.

However, I need to address this issue with the seriousness it deserves—there's nothing to be gained from acting as if this issue will be handled easily. The art of disagreeing without disrespect will be addressed in many of the following chapters, so I won't dive too deeply into it now. For now, though, I just want to introduce the idea that it is possible to have differing views without devolving into the hair-trigger, middle-finger discourse that is so common these days. Or worse, engaging in violent acts that could hurt or even kill another human being.

Most important, please don't think that I'm suggesting that we need to agree on everything or that we need to disagree less. If anything, I believe that one of the most useful things that we can do is to *disagree more*. Ending disagreements is not what we're going for here. The healthy debate of ideas, beliefs, and worldviews is how we grow and improve as a society, and we need more of that, not less. *It's how we're disagreeing that's the problem.*

We don't need to agree on everything, or anything really, but if we can refrain from disrespect, it could create an opening to find some common ground. Disrespecting someone, of course, demolishes any hope of finding it. Collectively, it's safe to say that our society will not survive unless we figure out how to disagree without disrespect, quickly.

Sounding the Alarm

When I peed in my pants, and on the floor, in my fifth-grade classroom, I craved things that didn't require money, time, or effort. Kindness. Compassion. Understanding. A supportive word. I received none of them.

Is it too much to ask a group of eleven-year-old children to show kindness, compassion, understanding, and a supportive word to the new kid who just peed on the floor? Maybe, but I don't think so. Now that I'm a father, I have seen extraordinary acts of kindness from my young daughters and their friends that have almost moved me to tears. Even if you believe that it's highly unlikely for children to resist the urge to laugh at a kid who peed on the floor, at the very least, hopefully, we can agree that my former teacher, who was the lone adult in the room, should have been able to provide some kindness if she was tethered to her humanity. Instead, she joined in on my classmates' laughter and created a scar that will remain with me for the rest of my life.

But this isn't about me; this is about you. It's about us. What if we could teach children the importance of kindness, compassion, and respect at an early age? We could literally create a new generation of kindness in the world. If we want that dream to become a reality, it's up to us as adults to model the behavior.

Civility matters, and we need to take action to restore our discourse now.

At the risk of being an alarmist, I'm going to sound the alarm, and if you choose to ignore it, the results could be catastrophic. Read on, if you don't believe me. If we don't take action, the risk will be inhabiting a world that could be worse than we could have ever imagined.

CHAPTER 2

The Abyss of Indifference

The opposite of love is not hate, it's indifference. The opposite of art is not ugliness, it's indifference. The opposite of faith is not heresy, it's indifference. And the opposite of life is not death, it's indifference.

—ELIE WIESEL

I want you to imagine something.

Picture a dystopian society where grown adults actively target the most vulnerable people among us: the disabled, the neurodivergent, the transgender community, the mentally ill, and people who are financially challenged. Instead of members of this society sharing kindness, support, or encouragement for these folks, this community has darker motives.

Their primary aim is to destroy these people.

Actually, that's not entirely accurate.

They want to relentlessly harass, stalk, defame, and emotionally abuse their victims until they ultimately feel compelled to destroy themselves. Some of their go-to techniques to achieve their goal include hijacking victims' social media accounts and using them as tools to irreparably destroy their reputations, doxing (the act of revealing identifying information about someone online, such as their real name, home address, workplace, phone, financial, and other personal information without the victim's consent), damaging their cherished relationships by unceasingly harassing their loved ones and family members, swatting (the deliberate and malicious act of reporting a false crime or emergency to evoke an aggressive law enforcement response, usually from a SWAT team), and even less sophisticated means like repeatedly mailing human feces to their victims.

And when they are successful in tormenting a victim to die by suicide, the members of this community revel in a twisted sociopathic glee and add a "+1" to their kill count. Similar to insatiable predatory animals hunting for prey in a darkened safari, they search frantically for their next victim, and ideally, for their next kill.

Let's pause for a moment.

If you're anything like me, you probably can't even begin to wrap your mind around this level of stupefying depravity. It would be understandable if you thought that you were reading the synopsis for an intensely unnerving horror movie script that would make the writers of *The Human Centipede* trilogy blush, but sadly, this is real life.

This community is known as Kiwi Farms, and it's an online forum that, from 2014 to 2022, was known for tormenting its targets into a helpless corner of submission, where death by suicide was the only option for finding peace. Tragically, Kiwi Farms has been implicated in the suicide deaths of at least three people[7] because of their unrelenting harassment, not to mention numerous attempted suicides, including Chloe Sagal, who lit herself on fire in a public park after enduring years of their abuse.[8]

In 2022, after ruining the lives of hundreds of people, their website was de-platformed from their web services and security provider. But like the mythical Hydra, once you think you killed it by cutting off one of its heads, two more heads will sprout in its place. Kiwi Farms may be dead as of this writing, but the hatefulness behind their toxicity is alive and well.

Alive and well.

Seriously, reflect on that for a moment. You and I share a world with people who are so deeply broken and hateful that they are mailing literal shit to people in hopes of ruining their lives, which likely is their least effective means of doing so. How does that make you feel? Angry? Disgusted? Scared? All of that is fine.

The only thing that we can't afford to feel right now is indifference.

---

7 Katelyn Burns, "My experience as a target of Kiwi Farms speaks to a scary truth about internet culture," September 10, 2022, https://www.msnbc.com/opinion/msnbc-opinion/kiwi-farms-made-internet-more-dangerous-trans-people-n1298815.

8 https://www.motherjones.com/politics/2023/02/kiwi-farms-die-drop-cloudflare-chandler-trolls/.

Indifference and the Shrug Squad

You might think that the Kiwi Farms example is extreme, and you would be right. However, you would be mistaken if you think extreme means that it's uncommon. These days, people who engage in behaviors and actions that are ruining lives are everywhere—they're in our neighborhoods, in our schools, in our churches, in our media, in our politics, and even in our own families. The tentacles of incivility have an unlimited reach, and it's worth examining how we got to this point before we get into the hard work of reversing this trend.

The answer is a simple one—indifference is how we got here. Indifference means having a lack of interest in or concern about something. Whether it is sitting in silence as a colleague is humiliated by her boss in a team meeting, shaking your head in exasperation as another mass shooting takes place in an elementary school and then going back to watching influencer videos on TikTok, or the countless Germans who witnessed their Jewish friends and neighbors endure unspeakable brutality and suffering from the Nazi regime during the Holocaust, indifference is the through line.

What does indifference look like? Have you ever seen the shrug emoji? It's the one where the avatar has a blank stare, elbows bent, and palms facing the sky. If shrug emojis could talk, they would say more than "I don't know" with their learned helplessness gesture. The shrug emoji avatar is also rhetorically asking, "And what do you want me to do about it?" In fact, when I picture real-life people offering a shrug to life's atrocities, the emoji's expressive shrug is almost too enthusiastic. Instead, the human shrug is usually just a half-hearted, one-inch raise and lowering of both shoulders, as they quickly process the information and then pitifully move on. If indifference were a sports team—besides going winless and being impossible to root for—their mascot would unquestionably be the shrug emoji.

You might not be aware of this, but indifference does have a team, and maybe you've found yourself in it before. The team is known as the Shrug Squad. These are the folks who resign themselves to accepting the awfulness of the world around them, actively convince themselves of their reduced agency to do something to change it, and weakly mumble phrases like "oh well," "that's so terrible," or "I'm sending thoughts and prayers" as they faithfully retreat to the glow of their connected devices to distract themselves from it. If that wasn't bad enough, the call to join the Shrug Squad is incredibly seductive. The Shrug Squad offers a warped sense of peace and self-preservation, but in reality, it provides neither. Sure, it may feel good to enjoy the temporary relief of not having to think or do anything about the world's problems, but the cost of this indulgence is unacceptably high. The reward for joining the Shrug Squad's team is a one-way ticket to our own demise as we join in on civility's death spiral as unwitting co-conspirators.

While all of this is true, the concept of indifference is too nuanced to be reduced to a simple conclusion that people need to pay attention and care more. There are some very legitimate reasons why people join the Shrug Squad, which I will address momentarily. However, I'm not including being a hateful bigot as a legitimate reason not to care about our fellow humans, because there's obviously nothing legitimate about that.

For the rest of us though, let's unpack three reasons why well-meaning people end up on the Shrug Squad so that we can hopefully shut down the team's open tryouts before anyone thinks of joining.

Reason #1: Overwhelmed with Stress

According to the American Psychological Association's (APA) *Stress in America 2023* report, Americans have a lot to be stressed out about. In their report, the APA listed the top stress-inducing concerns, and the percentages of adult participants who said those issues were significant sources of stress in their lives in 2023 are as follows:

- the future of our nation (68 percent)
- health-related stressors (65 percent)
- the economy (64 percent)
- money (63 percent)
- violence and crime (61 percent)
- the U.S. debt (57 percent)
- mass shootings (56 percent)
- social divisiveness (55 percent)
- healthcare (54 percent)[9]

Depending on which stressors you want to focus on, the reality is that many of them may get worse before they get better. As the stress mounts, these issues (and others not listed, such as family and marital challenges, toxic work environments, political divisiveness, discrimination, or wars abroad) can have an enormous effect on our overall health. Some of the physical signs of poorly managed stress include sleeplessness, high blood

9 American Psychological Association, "Stress in America 2023: A nation recovering from collective trauma," https://www.apa.org/news/press/releases/stress/2023/collective-trauma-recovery.

pressure, migraine headaches, irritable bowel syndrome, fertility challenges, depression, ulcers, unwanted weight gain, descent into addiction (food, drugs, alcohol, internet use, gambling, or pornography), post-traumatic stress disorder (PTSD), heart attacks, and potentially suicide, which brings up another big problem—according to the APA report, many people are not very skilled at managing their stress well:

- Sixty-two percent of adults said they don't talk about their stress overall because they don't want to burden others.
- Sixty-one percent said people around them just expect them to get over their stress.
- Thirty-six percent said they don't know where to start when it comes to managing their stress.
- Thirty-three percent said they feel completely stressed out no matter what they do to manage their stress.
- Forty-four percent said they don't feel anyone understands what they are going through.
- Fifty-two percent wish they had someone to turn to for advice and/or support.

My apologies, but there's more. If all of that wasn't enough, many people spend hours each day dealing with sneaky social media algorithms, alarmist cable news chyrons, and apoplectic political pundits screaming on satellite radio stations, which are all designed to keep us in a state of perpetual unhappiness and high stress.

OK, last point on this topic, I promise. Because of all of this, it's easy to fall into a state of fatalism. Fatalism is the belief that events are predetermined and inevitable, and our actions to alter those events won't make the smallest bit of positive difference. When we are dealing with overwhelming stress hitting us from all angles, the lure of a fatalistic mindset can feel like a very logical way to view the world. Unfortunately though, falling into a fatalistic state of helplessness and resignation about our circumstances will do nothing to improve those circumstances for ourselves or for others.

Whew! For people who love to worry, it's a fantastic time to be alive, isn't it?

Let's recap. First, Americans are significantly stressed about several things ranging from social divisiveness to the future of our country. Second, if that stress remains unchecked, it could present itself in several ways that will negatively affect our health and way of life (heart attacks, depression, or descent into addiction, to name a few). Third, according to the APA report, we aren't very good at acknowledging our stress or getting the help that we need. Fourth, many of us engage in drinking the toxic sludge from the fire hose of social media and cable news. And as we know, social media and cable news will happily provide us with blood-pressure-raising reminders of deadly wars abroad, political polarization, gun violence, racism, anti-Semitism, Islamophobia, homophobia, transphobia, and misogyny and how some of your fellow Americans are making your life a living hell. Lastly, all of the above have driven many people past indifference into a state of fatalism, where they feel powerless to do anything to make positive change.

Considering all of that, isn't it understandable that the last thing that people are going to be focused on are seemingly fluffy ideas around civility and respect? For many people, it's an ambitious goal just to make it to the safety of their bed at night with their sanity intact. Joining the Shrug Squad isn't a declaration of how little they care, but it's a declaration of their limited mental bandwidth to do something about it. In some cases, joining the Shrug Squad is a seemingly life-enhancing strategy to survive the emotional battering of toxic stress on a daily basis.

Reason #2: Someone Else Will Fix It

On March 13, 1964, one of the most infamous instances in American history of humanity's unwillingness to do the right thing took place.

After completing a late-night shift working at a local bar in New York City, Kitty Genovese drove home to her apartment to see her girlfriend and celebrate their first anniversary as a couple. Around three o'clock in the morning, as Kitty parked her car in front of her apartment building, a man named Winston Moseley brutally attacked her by stabbing her repeatedly with a large hunting knife.

Kitty screamed for help, which awoke some of the tenants in her apartment building, and her screams were enough to scare Moseley away. As she continued to call out for help, she eventually collapsed in front of the stairs to her apartment building due to her considerable injuries. Approximately ten minutes later, Moseley returned to the scene, and confident that no one was coming to help her, he proceeded to stab her again, rape her, and steal $49 from her before fleeing the scene. Kitty was pronounced dead shortly afterward.[10]

The reason why this story is infamous is not because of the evil of Winston Moseley (who, thankfully, was later caught and imprisoned). *This story made news because of the people who witnessed the brutal attack and chose to do nothing about it.* It was determined in a piece published by Martin Gansberg in *The New York Times* two weeks later that thirty-eight people sat and did nothing as this horrific crime unfolded. If even one of those people acted, there is a good chance that Kitty Genovese would have survived that vicious attack.

---

10 Charlotte Ruhl, "What happened to Kitty Genovese," August 3, 2023, https://www.simplypsychology.org/kitty-genovese.html.

Their response—or more accurately, their lack of one—is often referred to as the Bystander Effect. The Bystander Effect is a phenomenon where individuals are less likely to offer help to a person when there are other people present. This explains why the worst time for your car to break down on the side of the road is during rush hour.

This has dire implications in our collective fight to create a more civil world. There are nearly eight billion people on Earth right now. Surely, there are more educated, well-connected, and better-positioned people than you and me to tackle the issue of global incivility, right? Of course, there are. But using that logic, did the thirty-eight bystanders who witnessed Kitty Genovese's attack need to be off-duty police officers, trained mixed martial arts fighters, or be in possession of a stash of semiautomatic heat to take action against Winston Moseley to save her life? Of course not.

But still, it would be naïve to deny that the Bystander Effect isn't a seductive reason to join the Shrug Squad. Why put in the effort—or worse, potentially put ourselves at risk—if someone else can do it for us?

Reason #3: Easily Influenced Not to Care

In 1961, a young psychologist named Stanley Milgram conducted one of the most fascinating—and controversial—psychological studies in American history.

In hopes of understanding how everyday people were able to commit horrific acts of evil in Nazi Germany during the Holocaust, he crafted what is widely known as the Milgram obedience study. The goal was to see if people would remain obedient to an authority figure, even if the authority figure's orders conflicted with their personal values and moral beliefs. I remember learning about this for the first time in college, and I couldn't believe that it was real.[11]

The experiment involved three people: The Experimenter (a.k.a., the authority figure), the Teacher (the person whose behavior was being observed as the test subject), and the Learner. Both the Experimenter and the Learner were actors, which was unbeknownst to the Teacher. Participants in this experiment (specifically, the Teachers) were told that they were participating in a research project on learning and memory.

During the experiment, the Teacher was directed by the Experimenter to ask the Learner questions. The Learner was in an adjoining room, and when the Learner submitted an incorrect response, the Experimenter directed the Teacher to administer an electric shock to the Learner. It's important to note that before the experiment began, each of the Teachers was given a sample of the electric shock so that they would know firsthand the pain that they would be inflicting on the Learners.

With each wrong answer from the Learner, the voltage of the shocks increased in 15-volt increments, all the way up to a potentially life-ending 450 volts. Since the Learners were actors, they weren't actually being shocked when they submitted an incorrect answer to the Teacher's questions. Instead, tape-recorded responses would play, which included protests and banging against the adjoining wall—which only got louder and more desperate when the voltage increased. If the shock ever reached 450 volts, the Learner would become silent, which presumably meant that he was unconscious or dead.

Here's where it gets interesting. If the Teacher started getting weak in the knees and realizing that this was a terrible way to spend

---

11 Sprouts, "The Milgram experiment: would you do it?" https://www.youtube.com/watch?app=desktop&v=vuMt8b4Urcl.

a Saturday afternoon, the Experimenter would respond with four prompts, in this order:

1. *"Please continue."* If that didn't work, he would move on to prompt #2.
2. *"The experiment requires that you continue."* If that didn't work, he would move to prompt #3.
3. *"It is absolutely essential that you continue."* And finally, if that didn't work, then the final prompt.
4. *"You have no other choice, you must go on."*

The experiment ended only when the Experimenter exhausted all four prompts, or the Teacher administered the life-ending 450-volt shock to the Learner *three times*. Of all of the participants in Milgram's experiment, 100 percent of the Teachers administered a devastating shock of 300 volts to the Learners, and 65 percent of the Teachers administered the potentially fatal shock of 450 volts to the Learners. That experiment horrified me as a college freshman, and I hope that it raises the hairs on your neck too.

There's a lot to unpack here. Are our moral compasses so weakly calibrated that all it takes is for a charismatic authority figure to firmly tell us to do something horrific and we will do it without question? Similar to the wall between the Teacher and the Learner in Milgram's experiment, is it easier to hurt someone if we can't see their humanity? Unfortunately, in many cases, the answer to both questions seems to be "Yes."

It may be tempting to believe that we would behave differently if we were in the Teacher's seat in Milgram's experiment, but would we? History tells a different story. Whether it was the Holocaust, the transatlantic slave trade, Japanese internment camps, or lynchings and violence during the Jim Crow era, there were literally millions of "good" people who had a front-row seat to the worst atrocities in human history and chose to join the Shrug Squad.

Oftentimes, all it takes is for someone in authority to tell us that it's OK to behave in a way that runs counter to our values for us to accept the invitation to do it.

Indifference Is the Enemy

The call to join a helpless sea of indifference is deeply seductive, and in some cases, it seems like the only logical option. Whether it's succumbing to our overwhelming stress, being duped into the illusion that someone is going to fix this mess for us, or we cosign the bad faith argument made by authority figures (namely, politicians, cable news pundits, or social media influencers, to name a few) not to give a damn about our fellow humans, we will continue our slide into the abyss.

Unless we choose to do something about it.

I'm not expecting everyone to have the willingness or capability to escape indifference's grasp. The Shrug Squad has members in every country, town, neighborhood, and in some cases, household on Earth. This is going to be hard work and beginning in the next chapter until the end of the book, we'll get practical about how we're going to beat indifference and create a more civil world that we will be happy to leave to the younger generation after we're gone.

One thing is for sure, if we choose to do nothing, there may not be a world worth living in. Whether it's parents getting into fist fights at their kids' Little League games to the creation of Kiwi Farms, we need to do something to stop this. So, in other words, it's on us, my friend.

Let's talk about what we need to do.

CHAPTER 3

Killing the #1 Myth of Civility

Fight for the things that you care about, but do it in a way that will lead others to join you.

—RUTH BADER GINSBURG

There have only been two times in my adult life where I felt like I was going to break out in hives or literally throw up because of suffocating nervousness.

The first time was on December 29, 2008, when I rushed my wife Amber to the hospital to have an emergency C-section for the birth of my first daughter, Kaya, when the umbilical cord was wrapped around her neck. Thankfully, as of this writing, she's a thriving teenager who is embarrassed by my mere presence, so all is right with the world.

The second time was on September 23, 2021.

On that date, I was asked to testify in front of the Select Committee for the Modernization of Congress to share my ideas about how to bring more civility to Congress.

I'm assuming that you dropped this book on the floor during an uncontrollable fit of laughter because of anyone being dumb enough to try to "bring more civility to Congress," so I'll wait a few moments for you to compose yourself.

You good? OK, let's continue.

I get it—considering the current state of civility within the halls of Congress, I wouldn't blame you if you laughed yourself into a breathless stupor over the idea of getting these folks to act with more kindness and respect. The prevailing opinion is that the U.S. Congress is one of the most hopelessly dysfunctional bodies in the world, filled with lawmakers who are more interested in grandstanding on cable news stations than serving their constituents. That is likely why Congress' abysmally low approval ratings have not exceeded 25 percent in the past few years (even dropping as low as 13 percent approval in October 2023).[12]

---

12 Gallup, "Congress and the public," https://news.gallup.com/poll/1600/congress-public.aspx.

All of this was precisely why I was so nervous. Part of me felt like it was a setup. Who was I to offer any suggestions to these folks about being more respectful, compassionate, and kind to one another? If you asked me to crisply fold a fitted bed sheet or nail a piece of Jell-O to a tree, I would have found either of those to be a more reasonable ask. But since I love a challenge, I accepted the offer to fly out to Washington, DC, and spend two hours fielding questions from the lawmakers of the Select Committee with two other experts. It was an eye-opening day, for sure.

The Select Committee consisted of an equal number of Democrats and Republicans, which made it one of the only truly bipartisan committees in Congress. From my estimation, the lawmakers in attendance at the hearing were there in good faith, and they sincerely wanted to pull Congress out of the flames of the toxic dumpster fire of incivility and ineffectiveness that has been consuming their work for many years. Probably the biggest takeaway for me is that what we see on cable news or on social media is not representative of the behavior of many lawmakers on Capitol Hill. Even though as of this writing, the Select Committee for the Modernization of Congress is no longer an active committee, there remain responsible and serious lawmakers on both sides of the aisle who are working diligently behind the scenes to find remedies to bring sanity back to our politics. This is important for me to mention because stories about this kind of work rarely, if ever, make it onto national news.

After my time on Capitol Hill, the Select Committee staffers reached out to the folks who testified with any follow-up questions from the lawmakers. One of the questions was directed to me by Representative Nikema Williams, who serves Georgia's Fifth Congressional District. Here it is in its entirety:

My constituents sent me to Washington to get things done. They aren't looking for sound bites. They're looking for results. In Congress, you won't find me grandstanding. You'll find me working every lever in this institution to make sure the policy we pursue uplifts those most marginalized and creates a better life for the people of the Georgia's Fifth District.

In Congress, leadership does mean being collaborative. Today, the House is voting on my amendment to make sure the Small Business Administration regularly updates and distributes guidance to childcare providers on how to start and grow their small businesses. My co-leads on this amendment were Representative Pete Stauber from Minnesota and Representative Judy Chu from California. You won't find agreement on every issue among the three of us. But we all agree on this, and this is something that's going to make quality, affordable childcare more accessible. It'll be a benefit to our parents, kids, and economy—and something we couldn't have done without working together.

But make no mistake, leadership is about Good Trouble too. Leadership means always being true to your values and your constituents. I am always going to be out loud, on purpose on issues like strengthening our voting rights even if my Republican colleagues won't join me. I'll be collaborative with the partners I find and civilly—but vigorously—debate any colleagues who stand against what my constituents need.

Question: Mr. Richards, I think members have to make Good Trouble AND work collaboratively to get things done. Can you tell us a bit more about how members can successfully use both of these approaches to best represent and advocate for their constituents?[13]

13 Nikema Williams, Question for the Record from *Pathways to Success: How Practicing Civility, Collaboration, and Leadership Can Empower Members.* September 23, 2021, Congressional Session 117-10.

I'll address the question throughout the remainder of this book, but first, let's break down Representative Williams' statement. Before doing so, please put your political leanings aside for a moment, because that's not the point of me sharing this with you. Regardless of what side of the aisle you tend to hang out on, there is some useful guidance in Representative Williams' statement that we can and should use to our advantage.

There are three points specifically. First, Representative Williams, who is a Democrat, mentioned that she collaborated on an amendment with Representative Pete Stauber (a Republican) and Representative Judy Chu (a Democrat). She also wisely mentioned that they are not going to find agreement on all the issues, but they did find common ground on one important issue—namely, making quality and affordable healthcare more accessible. Representative Williams understood that in the halls of Congress, finding colleagues with whom you completely agree is an impossibility—whether those colleagues are on her side of the aisle or not. The same holds true in our families, workplaces, and friend groups as well. Needing to agree on everything before engaging in civil discourse with another human being is an exercise in immaturity and futility. The sooner that we can accept that we will inhabit the world with people who don't view it in the same way that we do, the better it will be for our society—not to mention, our mental health.

Second, Representative Williams said that she will be collaborative with the partners she finds while also vigorously debating the folks who stand against what her constituents need. Contrary to popular belief, the words "vigorously debating" are compatible with the concept of disagreeing without disrespect. Specifically, she noted that she will work collaboratively with the lawmakers who are open to the good faith exchange of ideas, and if not, and when necessary, she will be ready to debate those lawmakers with alacrity. This is the approach we must also take in our daily lives.

Third, her comment "I am always going to be out loud, on purpose on issues like strengthening our voting rights even if my Republican colleagues won't join me" might have struck a nerve with you if you're a Republican. Again, if this sentence caused you to wrinkle your nose in disgust, please don't allow your political leanings to cause you to dismiss the message. I'm confident that a Republican could say—and likely, has said—something similar about a Democrat. More importantly, one of the advanced skills on this civility journey is the ability to dispassionately separate the accurate parts of the message from our feelings about the messenger, which I appreciate is much easier said than done when politics are involved.

As Representative Williams showed, if it's possible in the halls of Congress to put up a spirited fight while still disagreeing without disrespect, then it can be done anywhere. Still though, there is a pervasive and persistent myth that civility means being passive, not putting up a fight, or weakly lowering our heads and accepting the worst aspects of our world as the way things have to be. Whether it's in my travels internationally as a speaker, at extended family gatherings, or during my workplace consultations, this myth seems to have incredible staying power.

So, I'm going to spend the rest of this chapter slaying this myth once and for all.

Civility in Unlikely Places

As a huge sports fan, one of the things that I love about professional sports is the intense competitive fire that burns within the athletes to win at all costs. Whether it's on the basketball court, football field, or baseball diamond, the athletes spend hours trying to defeat their opposition by any means necessary within the bounds of the rules. Being passive, weakly submitting to the other team's challenge, or helplessly throwing up their hands in surrender during the heat of competition is unthinkable to the athletes who play their sport at the highest level. They are there to win and, ideally, dominate.

While all of that is true, have you ever noticed what happens *immediately after a game*?

After the final out is recorded or the final seconds tick off of the game clock, the athletes from both sides usually converge at the midfield or at the half-court to hug the athletes they have been trying to demolish for the past two-plus hours. Some athletes trade their jerseys with their competitors, some pose for pictures, and some even join in prayer with their competitors.

It's a fascinating practice that deserves deeper inspection. Remember, this is the highest level of competition in the world. Let's just take my favorite professional sports league, the National Basketball Association (NBA), as an example. In a world of nearly eight billion people, there are only 450 active NBA players roaming the earth. Mathematically speaking, the odds of locking in one of those highly coveted spots is almost impossibly low, which makes the competition to join one of the most exclusive clubs on earth, incredibly fierce. In many cases, joining this exclusive club means acquiring generational wealth, a lifetime of fame and adoration, and the opportunity to become an all-time legend in the game that they have loved for their entire life. Yet still, after competing against someone who is indirectly trying to take one of those spots away from them, many are still willing to put their differences aside the moment the game ends.

In other words, professional athletes have unlocked a practice that has eluded many of us. They have discovered that it is possible to fight like hell while staying civil and respectful.

If the world of professional sports isn't high-enough stakes for you, what if we reenter the world of politics? On October 8, 2013, the former Republican governor of New Jersey, Chris Christie, and Democratic state senator Barbara Buono met in a televised gubernatorial debate. As far as televised political debates go, it wasn't particularly remarkable, except for one moment. The debate moderator asked the debate participants to say something that they liked about their opponent, and finally, things got a little interesting.[14]

Senator Buono went first and sarcastically quipped, "Well, he's good on late-night TV; he's just not so good in New Jersey."

Governor Christie followed Senator Buono's response by not taking the bait, and by using the art of civility, expertly. Calmly, he said, "She's obviously a good and caring mother and someone who cares deeply about public service in this state because she's dedicated a lot of her life to it. And while we have policy disagreements, I would never denigrate her service. And I think we need more people who care enough about our communities to be able to stand up and do the job that she's done over the last twenty years."

Can you imagine anything like this occurring on a debate stage today—or, anywhere in our current political landscape? In the cutthroat world of highly competitive politics where there can only be one winner, oftentimes, civility isn't even a consideration. Worse than that, in today's political climate, if a candidate offered that kind of civility to their opponent, that may cause them to *lose* the support of some voters instead of gaining it. However, in this instance, Governor Christie

14 https://www.latimes.com/opinion/opinion-la/la-ol-acts-of-political-kindness-20131212-photogallery.html.

proved that civility can be a winning strategy, and those who were in the debate hall felt a collective exhale after his comment. Many political pundits hailed his answer as the "knockout punch" in a race that he would go on to win handily by 22 percentage points a few weeks later. Who knew that there was such a thing as a civility knockout punch?

Was Governor Christie's comment about Senator Buono sincere? I have no idea, but the New Jersey voters seemed to think so. One veteran political commentator wrote about that moment after the debate by saying, "This was pretty skillful … I've been covering politicians for years … but even I think he might be at least partially sincere."[15]

Are the stakes *still* not high enough for you? OK, fair enough—what if I raised the stakes to life or death? Beginning on April 7, 1994, one of the most violent episodes in our world's history took place over the span of one hundred days in the small African country of Rwanda. The Rwandan majority population known as Hutu planned to kill the minority Tutsi population, and the genocidal results were horrifying.[16]

Between April and June 1994, nearly 800,000 Tutsis were massacred along with tens of thousands of Hutus. The brutality and cruelty were almost incalculable. School teachers gave up their own students for slaughter, neighbors turned against one another, and even family members viciously killed their own. The words on this page fail to adequately convey the prolific violence that occurred during those one hundred days, and for both participants and global observers, the idea that reconciliation could ever happen after the bloodshed was inconceivable.

As of this writing, it has been over thirty years since the Rwandan genocide, and the perpetrators and the victims of the violence are living side by side in peace. Isaie Nzeyimana, a professor of philosophy

---

15 Ibid.

16 CBC Radio, "Why Rwanda is held up as a model for reconciliation, 26 years after genocide," December 15, 2020, https://www.cbc.ca/amp/1.5842139.

at the University of Rwanda, spoke eloquently when he discussed the seemingly impossible task of reconciling after a genocide.

"Our country started from this premise: What if reconciliation between Rwandans was possible? Rwandans then acting from the assumption that reconciliation was indeed possible shifted the general dynamic. The Rwandan reconciliation is a model to follow because it has enabled Rwandans to understand one chapter of their history and begin to write a new one."[17]

And that's exactly what they did. Despite the process being complex and imperfect, the following are the initiatives that Rwandans have enacted since the genocide:

- Peace education to promote patriotism and fight against genocidal ideology
- Training of grassroots leaders, political party leaders, youth and women in trauma counseling, conflict mitigation, and early warning systems
- National summits on topics related to justice, good governance, human rights, national security, and national history
- Stating in the Constitution that all Rwandans have equal rights and passing laws to fight discrimination
- The National Unity and Reconciliation Commission has published a number of studies investigating the causes of conflicts in Rwanda and how to mitigate and resolve them[18]

There is so much power in professor Nzeyimana's words. What if we collectively decided to write a new chapter? What if we acted from

---

17 Ibid.

18 "The justice and reconciliation process in Rwanda," https://www.un.org/en/prevent-genocide/rwanda/pdf/bgjustice.pdf.

the assumption that *civility* is possible? If people can find a way to live peacefully next to someone who killed their family members, then I'm confident that we can find a way to live next to someone who plans to vote differently than we will in the upcoming election. Despite our deeply held passions and our bitter disagreements with the perceived other side, we can fight vigorously, and even when a line is crossed, reconciliation is possible as well.

Don't get it twisted, though. All I'm saying is that it's *possible*, not that any of this will be easy.

So, how do we do it? First, we'll have to kill a pesky myth that has incredible staying power.

The Ineffectiveness of Our Current Disagreements

First things first—civility is not about avoiding disagreements. The world will only improve by challenging the status quo. If anything, we need to disagree more. More skillfully, ideally. It's the robust exchange of ideas that holds the power to improve our families, our communities, and our policies and laws, and ultimately, the country and the world.

This persistent myth that being civil means constantly turning the other cheek, being passive, or remaining neutral on issues that matter to you is flat out wrong. Generational challenges, such as systemic inequities, will never be solved with that dangerously naïve mindset. For example, let's take a very divisive issue where civility is difficult.

Abortion.

The typical way that both sides discuss this polarizing topic could look like this:

Person A: "I'm so happy that we're finally waking up as a country and starting to end the horrific act of killing babies. I hope you're with me on this."

Person B: "Killing babies … seriously? That is a ridiculous mischaracterization, and you know it. Maybe you should consider putting your Bible down for a minute and crack open a biology book. More importantly, you have no right to tell me what I can do with my own body. How about this for a novel idea? If you're against abortion, then don't have one."

Person A: "You are a monster. You're basically saying that it's cool to kill innocent lives because you're too reckless, or too stupid, to engage in basic birth control. Or, how about this for a novel idea? Keep your legs closed. People like you are sick in the head and I hope that all of you murderers mercilessly burn in a lake of fire in the deepest recesses of hell."

Person B: "Awfully judgmental, isn't it? Doesn't your silly holy book frown on that type of behavior? Since we're judging each other—you and your brain-dead, cult-follower nonsense is making my skin crawl. Get a grip—it's the twenty-first century, not the Stone Ages. The agency over my body is my right, and there's no way that I'm going to let you, or any other regressive Jesus-freak nut job, take that away from me."

Well, damn.

The problem is that there are many people who believe that this is the only way to discuss issues that are extremely polarizing. If you don't believe me, visit the comment section of any social media post that's discussing a controversial topic. Out of all of the polarizing topics on the table, abortion is one of the most emotionally fraught ones in existence today. In order for discussions about this issue not to slide into the abyss of incivility or worse, we need to have a simple strategy that we can pull out in a moment's notice.

I'll get to that strategy later in this chapter, but first, we must address an invisible force that is making our lives harder.

Entropy and Intentional Consistent Interventions

You might not be aware of this, but there is a concept that is based on the second rule of thermodynamics that is affecting all of us in some way. Don't worry, I'm not capable of nerding out too hard on physics, so I promise that this will only be a brief departure from my civility lane. The very high-level summary of the second law of thermodynamics is that all things naturally trend from a state of order to disorder. The word for this is entropy, and the examples of this are countless.

If you were to take a brand-new deck of perfectly ordered playing cards and dump them to the ground, you've just created disorder. Leaving the playing cards to their own devices, the likelihood that the deck of cards will become *even more disordered* is high, whereas the chances of the cards regaining their original ordered state without some sort of intervention are extremely low. The previous sentence is important, so kindly keep it in mind as you read on.

Moving on from the deck of playing cards metaphor to things that actually affect our daily lives, the creep toward disorder affects everything.

Without consistent small interventions, entropy will slowly and effectively nudge the things that you care about closer to a state of chaos. The cleanliness of your home will gradually descend into a dust-coated, disordered mess. Your marriage, your friendships, and your relationships with your kids and loved ones will trend toward dysfunction. The cells in your body will naturally degrade over time and negatively affect your health. Your workplace culture will devolve into a noxious sea of toxicity and abuse. Your once-sharpened memory will fade into a scattered mess. And yes, our social discourse will devolve into incivility, disrespect, and personal attacks. In fact, we're already there.

Unfortunately, entropy is both inevitable and invincible. Even though almost everything trends toward disorder, we can still manage it, even if we can't stop it. And similar to picking up the scattered deck of playing cards on the ground and putting them back in order, we will need to apply intentional energy to the things that matter in our lives in hopes of regaining order.

I like to call these small acts *intentional consistent interventions* (ICIs, for short). They're intentional, meaning that we have decided to take deliberate and thoughtful action to slow the disorder of entropy. They're consistent, meaning we must continue to give our best effort to repeatedly taking those deliberate actions until the day we die. And lastly (and most important), the intervention is all about the act of interfering with a potential undesirable outcome, which is exactly what we're hoping to do.

Here are some examples of some ICIs that you may be applying in your everyday life right now.

- Consistently organizing and cleaning your bedroom to maintain the order of a tidy sleeping space

- Consistently nourishing your relationships with respect and kindness, meaningful conversation, quality time together, and empathic support during hard times to maintain the order of a healthy interpersonal connection
- Consistently eating well and moving your body to maintain the order of good health
- Consistently rewarding desired actions in your workplace and holding people accountable for undesirable behaviors to maintain the order of a healthy work culture
- Consistently learning new skills (a foreign language, playing a musical instrument, or new hobby), reading thought-provoking books, and engaging in creative endeavors (writing, art, or music) to maintain the order of a sharp mind

It could be argued that since entropy is undefeated, what's the point of fighting against it? That would be like saying, "What's the point in showering? We're only going to get dirty again." These ICIs will not stop entropy from occurring, but they will go a long way in slowing down the decline into disorder and staving off undesirable results for as long as possible. In the case of our civil discourse, where we are already mired in a disordered state, engaging in ICIs will be the most effective means of turning the tide. One thing is for sure—doing nothing or disrespecting and hating our fellow humans will only succeed in adding to the problem that we are hoping to fix.

In addition, some sobering words of caution. The level of disorder will determine the amount of energy that must be expended to regain order. In other words, the amount of energy that it will take to reorganize a deck of playing cards into its original ordered state after you drop it to the ground will be far less than the amount of energy it will take to return a shattered egg that you dropped on the ground back to its original ordered state.

Not that you need me to tell you this, but our current state of civil discourse is more like the shattered egg than the deck of playing cards, but that doesn't mean that we can't put Humpty Dumpty back together again. It's just going to take a great deal of intentional and consistent effort to make it happen.

Disagreeing Strategically

So, where should we intentionally place our effort to slow the force of entropy in our discourse? To answer that, let's revisit the abortion discussion.

Both sides have strong views; they are both passionately entrenched in their diametrically opposed positions, and emotions are high—all of which is a perfect recipe for a disastrous outcome. One example of an ICI is to use ground rules, which will set the parameters for the discussion and lay the groundwork to disagree more strategically.

Let's see it in action from both sides of the argument.

Scenario 1

Person A: "I'm so happy that we're finally waking up as a country and starting to end the horrific act of killing babies. I hope you're with me on this."

Person B: "Before I respond, I know that a lot of these discussions about abortion can go off the rails pretty quickly. Can we agree to stay respectful, even if my opinion is different from yours?"

OR

Scenario 2

Person B: "These brain-dead cult followers are trying to bring us back to the Stone Ages by removing our right to choose. I hope you're with me on putting a stop to their foolishness."

Person A: "Before I respond, I know that a lot of these discussions about abortion can go off the rails pretty quickly. Can we agree to stay respectful, even if my opinion is different from yours?"

Let's break down this ICI into its three important parts:

The first part is to acknowledge to the other party that we're about to wade into dangerous waters where the discourse can devolve in a hurry. It's an important reminder and will raise the other person's awareness that if the discussion becomes disrespectful, it will be because one of the two of them crossed that line. Ideally, that person won't be you.

The second part is asking them a simple "yes-or-no" question to see if they are capable of disagreeing without disrespect. You are setting the terms of how this conversation will go, and based on the other person's answer, it will determine if it even goes forward at all. The power in this is that you have challenged the other person to engage in a highly polarizing topic, respectfully.

The third part is deciding if it's worth continuing forward with the conversation. At this point, anything short of a "yes" response is not worthy of your engagement. For example:

Scenario 1 or Scenario 2—Response #1

Person A *or* Person B: "Sure, I guess. I'm not sure how any respectful person would have a different opinion, though."

Person B *or* Person A: "I do have a different opinion. Are you open to hearing it?"

Person A *or* Person B: "Not really."

At this point, disengage.

Scenario 1—Response #2

Person A: "I have no respect for anyone who thinks that murder is an acceptable practice, so if that's where you're going with this, then save your breath. You will be judged harshly, and I hope God has no mercy on your wretched soul."

Person B: "To be clear, I don't think that murder is an acceptable practice. I'm happy to get into this more deeply, but as I asked earlier, are you willing to stay respectful even if my opinion is different from yours?"

Person A: "Are you insane? If you're pro-murder, then there's no respectful ground for us to begin from. We're done here."

OR

Scenario 2—Response #2

Person B: "I have no respect for anyone who thinks that they have the right to control my body, so if you're thinking about waving your holy book at me, save your energy. My body, my choice."

Person A: "I have no interest in waving a holy book at you. I'm happy to get into this more deeply, but as I asked earlier, are you willing to stay respectful even if my opinion is different from yours?"

Person B: "Did I stutter? If you think you can control my body, then there's no respectful ground for us to begin from. We're done here."

Again, in both of the scenarios, if you're receiving Response #2, it's also time to disengage.

Surprisingly, there are some subtle benefits to both of the first two responses. You have demonstrated the rare willingness to engage in a polarizing topic, respectfully. You invited the person to have a civil discussion, and they chose not to do so. They will have to live with the fact that they were not up to the task of modeling impulse control, emotional maturity, and a willingness to find common ground.

The first two responses failed to get us what we were looking for. Here's how it could play out when we receive the "Yes" response we desire.

Scenario 1—Response #3

Person A: "Yes, of course."

Person B: "I believe strongly in my right as a woman to choose what happens within my own body."

Person A: "But what about the fetus? Doesn't the fetus have rights too? Why are your rights more important?"

Person B: "Science hasn't determined that life begins at conception, but my life is 100 percent verifiable. Because of that, I have the right to make decisions that are right for me, and I believe that every woman should have the right to do the same."

Person A: "I don't make my decisions based on what scientists discover in a laboratory. I make my decisions based on my faith, morality, and common sense. Voluntarily killing a baby with a beating heart is simply barbaric and inexcusable."

Person B: "But what if the life of the mother was at risk? What if a woman was raped? What if a minor was the victim of incest? In those cases, I feel that it is barbaric and inexcusable to remove the choice from the woman—or *the girl*—who needs to do what is best for her health and quality of life going forward."

OR

Scenario 2—Response #3

Person B: "Yes, of course."

Person A: "I believe strongly that all lives should be honored and cherished. That happens to be my faith, but to be clear, you don't need to be religious to think this way. There may be extreme examples, like when the mother's health is at risk, but generally speaking, I believe that the act of abortion should be outlawed."

Person B: "But, why is that your call? Why should you, or some politician in Washington, DC, have any say over what I do with my body?"

Person A: "I'm advocating for a life that doesn't have a voice. The life that is in a mother's womb is not able to fight for themselves, so I feel called to fight for them."

Person B: "Doesn't that just make you 'pro-birth' and not 'pro-life'? It seems like the focus is on controlling women's bodies and getting us to give birth, and then when the kid is born, y'all seem to lose interest in the kid or the mom. It's bizarre to me."

Person A: "I don't see it that way at all. All lives are important, both inside and outside of the womb. And as I mentioned, if the life of the mother was at risk, then I could understand making that decision, because a life is at stake. But in other situations, such as unwanted pregnancies, there are other options, particularly adoption, where the child could have a shot at a beautiful and loving life."

The Power of Civil Discourse

I'll stop here, because I could use the remainder of this book playing out this discussion on both sides.

Notice two things—the first is that neither side backed down and their opinions stayed as strong as ever. Second, when both parties agree to stay respectful at the beginning, that will increase the likelihood that they will stay respectful throughout their disagreement. Of course, we are talking about human nature here, and it's possible that emotions will rise and the whole conversation could derail. If that happens with the other person, then remind them of your agreement before continuing. However, if you are the one who is losing your cool, then you'll need to learn the art of emotional regulation, which we will discuss in the next chapter.

Our primary objective in this work is to keep our eyes on the prize by keeping the main thing the main thing—which is enhancing the quality of our discourse. It's doubtful that one respectful discussion is going to change the other person's mind, especially when it comes to a topic like abortion. But what if it's not about changing minds in the moment, winning the argument, or owning the other side? Maybe the bigger goal is to potentially open a person's mind to the other side of the argument in a respectful way? On the contrary, it is guaranteed that no minds will be opened if we are shouting down, shaming, or disrespecting other people. That's why this ICI of setting ground rules before diving into a polarizing topic like abortion, gun control, politics, and the like can be a helpful tool to slow the slide into toxic discourse.

As mentioned, I plan on sharing many more ICIs in this book. And while "Setting the Ground Rules" is effective for polarizing discussions—meaning that there are two sides worthy of debate—this particular ICI wouldn't be effective when addressing racism, anti- Semitism or Islamophobia (where there aren't two sides worthy of debate).

For now, let's lay to rest the myth that civility means that we can't fight like hell for what we believe in. You can and you should. However, to intervene against the absurdly high entropy of our current discourse, we must lead the way by showing that we can fight respectfully and model the way for others to do the same.

The foundation has been laid, which is the easy part. You are ready my friend, to begin the work.

Intentional Consistent Interventions Overview

From this point forward, at the end of each chapter, there will be a section dedicated to ICIs. The goal of *Civil Unity* is to be a practical book where we will actively apply the concepts in these pages into our lives, and the ICIs are designed to do exactly that.

As a reminder, ICIs are:

1. **I**ntentional: we must take deliberate and thoughtful action to slow the disorder of entropy.
2. **C**onsistent: we must continue to give our best effort by repeatedly taking those deliberate actions until the day we die.
3. **I**nterventions: we must actively use our intentional and consistent actions to interfere with a potential undesirable outcome.

As noted, the *C* in ICI stands for consistent, so applying an ICI once or twice will not make a meaningful difference any more than doing one set of bicep curls will make a difference to our physiques. The consistent practice of these exercises is what is required, and you will be asked to apply each ICI whenever you encounter a particular situation, over a designated period of time, or even every day.

To get the most out of the ICI process, you will need your own private *Civil Unity Journal* to keep track of your progress. This doesn't need to be anything fancy—you could use a typical journal that can be purchased from a bookstore, or you can use a regular notebook. However, to make things easier for you, I have created a PDF version of the *Civil Unity Journal* that is available as a companion guide for download on my website: www.civilunitybook.com.

Most important, uniting the world around the idea of civility is not a spectator sport—we need to actively get into the game, and I hope that you're ready to join me. If so, let's jump into the first of the twenty-six ICIs in this book.

INTENTIONAL CONSISTENT INTERVENTION #1: *SETTING THE GROUND RULES*

Before entering into a polarizing conversation, set the parameters of the discussion.

ICI Steps:

1. Acknowledge that you are about to enter into a conversation where emotions could run high and the discourse could derail: "Before I respond, I know that a lot of these discussions about the security of our southern border can go off the rails pretty quickly."
2. Ask the other party a simple "yes-or-no" question to see if they are willing to engage in a discussion about a controversial topic, respectfully: "Can we agree to stay respectful, even if my opinion is different from yours?"
3. If you receive anything less than a "yes," feel free to disengage. If you do receive a "yes," then continue the discussion. Also, if during the conversation, the other party starts to fall into the tempting trap of disrespect, remind them of your shared agreement. After your reminder, if they cannot continue the conversation without personal attacks and insults, then simply disengage.
4. In your *Civil Unity Journal*, answer the following questions:
    - Was setting ground rules easier than you thought it would be, harder than you thought it would be, or was it what you expected? Why?

- Were you able to remain respectful while vigorously debating the polarizing topic? Was the other party able to do the same? Did establishing ground rules improve the overall quality of the discussion?
- Were there any lessons learned after the discussion? Was there anything that you will do differently next time you engage in a polarizing conversation?

PART 2

THE WORK

CHAPTER 4

The Inner Work

Caring for myself is not self-indulgence, it is self-preservation and that is an act of political warfare.

—AUDRE LORDE

A quick recap before pushing forward.

In chapter 1, we discussed what civility is and why it's important. In chapter 2, we discussed succumbing to indifference and why it can be so easy to join the Shrug Squad and the terribly high cost of doing so. And in chapter 3, we dispelled the myth that civility means we can't passionately *and* respectfully fight for our beliefs. Chapter 3 also introduced the invincible power of entropy and how this force can be managed with ICIs.

Now that the foundation has been laid, it's time to get to the hard stuff. In other words, it's time to do the work.

Let's start with the part of the civility work that is often ignored—what is going on in between our two ears. As mentioned in chapter 2, the pull toward indifference is a strong one. The influences that want us to suit up for the Shrug Squad are everywhere, so we're going to have to use some *ICIs* (sorry, reinforcement is a critical teaching tool) to ensure that entropy doesn't slowly push us into the abyss of incivility.

To understand why we must begin our work here, I'm going to share with you a painfully obvious truth: there are some very difficult people who we will have to deal with in this world. Unless we choose to hide under our beds for the rest of our lives and disavow the rest of the human race, we will have no choice but to navigate a world with self-centered narcissists, toxic bullies, sociopathic gaslighters, unabashed bigots, and soulless monsters who delight in the unnecessary inclusion of raisins into cakes and pies.

We will never be able to rid ourselves of these people, so it's up to us to prepare for them and effectively manage our responses to their behavior. The starting point of uniting behind a more civil world begins with us being fully ready for what's waiting for us, and it begins with resilience.

Building Resilience and Tough Love Self-Care

Have you ever wondered how some people are able to become stronger after enduring life-shattering adversity like the death of a child, infidelity of a spouse, the loss of a limb, sexual assault, or the diagnosis of a serious disease, while some people have their entire day ruined because their meal at a restaurant was prepared incorrectly?

The difference is resilience.

Resilience is defined as our ability to withstand, or recover quickly from, difficult or unpleasant circumstances. To be clear, this is not to say that the folks who experienced wildly difficult circumstances bounced back immediately after the unexpected death of a loved one, for instance. Resilient people don't have hidden superpowers that are inaccessible to the rest of us or are able to turn off their emotions like a finely tuned robot. They experience emotional anguish and devastation just like most people, but they have also discovered skills—whether intentionally or unintentionally—that anyone can learn to recover more quickly than the average person.

It is essential that we intentionally discover these skills too, because as mentioned, we will encounter rude, thoughtless, and mean-spirited people throughout our civility journey. If we allow the experiences with those folks to harden our hearts and write off the human race as irredeemable, what are the odds of us behaving in a civil manner toward anyone? However, if we can remain resilient and not allow a negative experience (or possibly, a series of negative experiences) to close our hearts, we will be more likely to bounce back from those unpleasant experiences to build connections with others. In other words, if we choose the path of resilience, then we get to maintain our agency by choosing how we interact with the world. If we choose the opposite, then our mood, our attitude, and our mindset will be determined by how the world chooses to interact with us. Only one of those options will get us closer to a more civil society.

In the past decade, after talking to my workshop participants, email list subscribers, social media followers, friends, and family—some of whom are the most resilient people on earth—it's clear that they do things differently from nonresilient people. When examining the most resilient people I have known in my lifetime, they do engage in self-care activities like going to the spa or relaxing with a good book (which I highly recommend for our mental health), but they also engage in something I like to call "Tough Love Self-Care." Unlike going to the spa, Tough Love Self-Care involves the necessary (and sometimes, unpleasant) self-care actions we must take to strengthen our minds and our bodies for the difficult challenges ahead.

Engaging in Tough Love Self-Care accomplishes two things, simultaneously; it creates the needed space in our lives to combat overwhelm and discontent, and it proves to ourselves that we are capable of doing hard things, like uniting our world around civility. The following are some Tough Love Self-Care actions that some of the most resilient people alive use to reduce overwhelm and enhance their mental strength.

Maintaining Healthy Boundaries and Saying "No"

If you are consistently overscheduled, overwhelmed, and just plain exhausted all of the time, it is OK to put yourself first and say "No" to the unnecessary activities that are taking up your discretionary time. Oftentimes, people tell me that they say "yes" when they want to say "no" because they don't want to appear selfish, or they don't want to deal with an awkward or difficult conversation that may come after a boundary is enforced. I've found that you can learn a lot about a person based on how they respond to you enforcing healthy boundaries. Usually, people show respect by saying, "I totally understand. Props to you for respecting your boundaries." Then, there are the ones who get angry, freeze you out, or try to make you feel guilty. When you encounter those people, remember this: the only people who will be upset with you enforcing your boundaries are the people who benefited from you not having any boundaries in the first place.

It is impossible to lead a healthy and balanced life—not to mention, do the hard work of fighting for civility—if you don't have clear boundaries that you are willing to enforce.

Removing Yourself from Toxic Relationships

Consider this addition by subtraction. If you have someone in your life who brings you constant drama, headaches, and misery, and your eyes roll to the back of your head whenever you see their name pop up on your cell phone's caller ID, you may need to compassionately cut them loose from your life. In some cases, that may not be possible, but if so, at the very least, limit your interactions with them as much as possible. It will be exceedingly difficult to navigate the challenges of creating a more civil world if you allow a habitually draining, unkind, and potentially harmful person to remain in your inner circle.

Some people in our lives need to be loved from a distance.

Prioritizing Rest and Fully Unplugging While on Vacation

Rest is not earned. You deserve rest, which includes taking vacations, sleeping eight hours a night, and enjoying leisure time, because you are a human being. There is nothing honorable about working around the clock, staying late at work, and refusing to take vacations (and when you do, you're working the entire time anyway). This work is draining—mentally, physically, emotionally, and spiritually—that's why committing to rest and recovery is not a luxury, but it's a survival requirement.

And on a cautionary note for my workaholics, remember this to maintain a healthy perspective: twenty years from now: the only people who will remember you staying late at the office and working on vacations are your loved ones and your friends.

Making Healthy Food Choices and/or Exercising

Can you imagine an hour before running an ultramarathon that we chose to devour a half-dozen bacon-covered doughnuts, a pack of Twizzlers, and wash it down with a two-liter of Mountain Dew and a shot of whiskey? Terrible idea, right? With that kind of fuel, we are almost guaranteeing a suboptimal performance and a crash that could make it onto the nightly news. I believe that we need to view the journey of creating a more civil world in the same way as if we were running an ultra. It's going to be challenging and stressful, and numerous times along the way, everything within us will scream at us to quit. Being resolute in our purpose will provide us an excellent foundation, but it's the quality of our fuel that will keep us going. Choosing nutrient-dense foods, staying hydrated, and, if able, moving our bodies will make an enormous difference if our goal is to maintain the stamina to keep pushing forward for as long as possible.

Forgiving Others (and Yourself, If Necessary)

I will unpack this in more depth in chapter 9, but for now, allow me to address what is parenthetically mentioned previously.

Self-forgiveness is hard work, and unfortunately, it's something that many people don't choose to do. If we are constantly judging ourselves harshly, beating ourselves senseless after any mistake, and demanding perfection, this is going to be a brutal slog for us. Despite our best intentions, we will engage in conversations where we will say the wrong thing, make bad situations worse, and potentially damage relationships that matter to us. Are you good with that? I hope so, because unless you have the superhuman social skills of Yoda, the Dalai Lama, or Mr. Rogers, you are not going to do this perfectly, and neither will I.

The ability to forgive ourselves is not only a powerful resilience skill, but it will prove useful as we actively engage in creating a more civil world.

Asking for Help and/or Reaching Out to a Therapist

I cannot even imagine attempting to navigate this world without my therapist.

Having a nonjudgmental space for me to express my fears, insecurities, disappointments, and deepest feelings is one of the greatest gifts that I have on this journey. My ability to manage my stress has increased exponentially with my therapist in my life, and as mentioned in chapter 1, I've been able to work through some deeply repressed trauma that ran like a malicious virus in the back of my mind for decades.

In addition, as a Black man in America, I had to overcome quite a bit of negative stigma and programming just to reach out to a therapist. For years, I heard from woefully misguided people that "therapy is for crazy white folks" and that I needed to "man up and quit being a punk." Needless to say, neither of those pieces of advice did a damn thing to improve my fading mental health.

I do understand that not everyone is fortunate enough to have access to quality mental healthcare. If you can reach out to a trusted friend or even a hotline, anything is better than nothing. However, if you have the resources and it's the stigma that you're fighting against, please realize a couple of things: It's OK not to be OK, and your mental health is part of your overall health. Don't let outdated and dusty old ideas around mental wellness stop you from getting the help you need.

These Tough Love Self-Care tactics are practical and simple (not easy, *simple*) ways to ensure that we are working from a solid foundation of resilience as we do this work. However, we'll need more than Tough Love Self-Care to ensure that we won't end up on the Shrug Squad as mentioned in chapter 2. Speaking of the Shrug Squad, let's address each of the three reasons why someone could end up on that team and what we must do to prevent it.

1. How to Address "Being Overwhelmed by Stress"

There is a misconception that resilience is formed in a place of rugged individualism and superhuman grit, but nothing could be further from the truth. This world is too challenging to effectively navigate it on our own, and it's only when we decide to lean into the willing help of others that we will become resilient. I like to call this process "Building Your Crew," and it's one of the most effective ways to deal with the overwhelming nature of toxic stress.

The power of a strong support system has been lauded throughout history, and it is credited for helping people to overcome extreme trauma ranging from crippling addictions to the death of a child to sexual assault. There is something magical and wildly effective about leaning on the healing power of finding a tribe of folks who have endured similar pain.

This tactic is especially helpful if we're hoping to stay resilient in the face of incivility. Here are three characteristics of people you should have in your inner circle (a.k.a., your crew) to inspire you to keep going as you work to create a more civil world.

Someone Who Will Feel with You

Empathy is the ability to understand another person's thoughts and feelings in a situation from their point of view rather than your own. Having someone in your crew who is empathetic and is willing to create a psychologically safe environment to feel your highs and lows with you can be extremely cathartic. I can promise you this—if you have decided to commit to the active demonstration of respect toward others, and the ability to disagree without disrespect, it won't protect you from people who will give nary a damn about your civility commitments.

If your boss just eviscerated you in front of your team, your neighbor just purposefully kicked her dog out of anger, or if there's a hate rally that's marching through the main street in your town, you may understandably feel like hopelessly throwing up your hands and giving up on trying to create a more civil world. But it's exactly at this point where having an empathic ear in your crew can help you to remain resilient and stay the course.

Whether it's a trained professional like a therapist, a trusted friend, or a loved one, it is crucial to have someone with you on this journey who is willing to feel with you. Not only will it help you to offload some unhelpful negative energy, but it will also remind you that you're not alone in feeling like you do, and most of all, it will give you hope that others care as much about this work as you do.

Someone Who Will Laugh with You

The ability to laugh at the world, and at ourselves, is another trait of the resilient. Viktor Frankl, the Austrian neurologist and psychiatrist who survived the Holocaust in Nazi Germany, wrote the following in his book, *Man's Search for Meaning*, "Humor was another of the soul's weapons in the fight for self-preservation. It is well known that humor, more than anything else in the human makeup, can afford aloofness and an ability to rise above any situation, even if only for a few seconds."[19] If anyone in our world's history is qualified to talk about resilience, it's Mr. Frankl.

19 Viktor Frankl, *Man's Search for Meaning* (Boston, Ma.: Beacon Press, 2006).

Humor doesn't mean that we should be laughing ourselves into a stupor when contemplating our own suffering or when viewing the suffering of others. That would make us at best a little weird and, at worst, completely sociopathic. But what if we can briefly tap into the absurdity of a situation and reframe it for the ridiculousness that it is? Better yet, we should intentionally seek out people in our crew who have a sense of humor, so they can remind us of this fact when we may be too lost in the struggle to see it for ourselves.

It may surprise you that some professions, such as hospice nurses, crisis counselors, and social workers, often rely on the power of humor to help them get through their days. If not, the vicarious trauma and the heaviness of the work that they are engaged in daily would likely destroy them. Building a more civil world is heavy work too, and we will need to engage in the power of laughter and humor to stay the course.

And for real—if Viktor Frankl can find meaning and humor in the depths of a Nazi concentration camp, we can probably find meaning too in our daily struggles, if we try hard enough.

Someone Who Will Stand with You

If you're a parent, you will likely remember the brutal period shortly after your bundle of joy was born where you were sleep deprived, on edge, and full of anxiety about how you were going to keep the tiny human who is now under your care alive. Somehow, you were able to tap into some source of energy to keep pushing through, even though every fiber in your body was screaming at you to fall face first into your bed.

The reason why is because we were connected to a purpose that was bigger than ourselves and bigger than the transitory challenges that we were experiencing at the time. Resilient people realize that while that is true, our energy is finite. We will need others who will stand with us on our journey to remind us of the importance of our long-term positive intention, our efforts, and the potential impact we will have if we continue (and the consequences if we quit). Whether it was Harriet Tubman, Helen Keller, or Nelson Mandela, the most resilient people the world has ever known were all resolute in their purpose.

If we are equally committed to our purpose of creating a more civil world, we will need folks in our crew who will stand with us and remind us that this challenging work is worthwhile.

Most of all, resilient people understand that they don't have to figure everything out by themselves. Intentionally and consistently intervening against entropy and incivility by building a strong crew can be the difference between joining the Shrug Squad and potentially saving the world.

Building Your Crew

Building a crew is mandatory to stay the course in creating a more civil world. At minimum, it is required to have people in your network who will feel with you when you're struggling, laugh with you when things get heavy, and stand with you when you need to be reminded of the importance of your purpose.

If you already have people in your network who meet the criteria, your job is to do everything in your power to reinforce and enhance those relationships. If you currently don't have people in your life who meet the criteria, that's OK. There are some practical ways to find and create relationships that will enhance your life.

Explore Your Interests

Do you love video games? Sports teams? Hiking? International travel? Knitting? Fitness? Cooking? Book clubs? Whatever your interests may be, there are numerous groups (both online and offline) where there are countless people who share the same passion for your area of interest that you do. This is a fantastic way to meet like-minded people and, ideally, people who share the same interest in civility too. To help in this effort, I have created a private *Civil Unity* Facebook group where you can meet other people who share your passion to create a more civil world and engage in in-depth conversations with them.

Volunteer Your Time

I've found that some of the kindest people I have ever met were the ones who were willing to donate their time in the service of their fellow humans. It could be anything from assisting people experiencing homelessness, refereeing youth sports games, cleaning up the local community, or making meals for people less fortunate. If you do choose to donate your time, you are almost guaranteed to make meaningful connections as you work closely with others, grow personally, discuss shared interests and challenges, and become a more well-rounded individual.

Stay the Course

There is no magic formula when it comes to finding people who will become part of your crew, and it may take time. It's easy to become discouraged, but please don't quit. There are nearly eight billion people on this planet, and I am willing to say confidently (and admittedly, unscientifically) that at least a quarter of those folks are fiercely passionate about creating a more civil world. You just have to find them. As mentioned, if you don't know where to start, join my *Civil Unity* Facebook group.

2. How to Address "Someone Else Will Fix It"

I don't have the blueprint for happiness, but I do know the one for extreme misery. The unhappiest people I know are the ones who constantly try to control aspects of their lives that are completely outside of their control. As simple as this concept is, it is far from easy, because if it were, everyone would be doing it. The most resilient people on earth understand the importance of controlling the controllables in their lives, and instead of fighting against the things that they cannot change (or worse, expecting others to fix our problems for us), they choose acceptance.

Acceptance is often misunderstood. It has nothing to do with resigning yourself to tolerate the worst aspects of the world, showing approval for the undesirable circumstances you're in, or pretending that you're not sad, angry, or devastated by what you're going through. Acceptance simply means that you are fully acknowledging that the situation is beyond your control, in hopes of releasing the situation's control over your sanity, your well-being, and your life.

A great example of this is the story of surfing prodigy, Bethany Hamilton. At the age of thirteen while surfing off the coast of Hawaii, she was attacked by a fourteen-foot tiger shark and lost her left arm. While that traumatic moment would have understandably broken most people—and definitely most teenagers—Bethany was back in the water just a few weeks later. Within two years of the attack, she had won her first surfing national championship and would go on to become one of the best surfers in the world.

Let's break this down for a moment. In her first year as a teenager, while enjoying the sport that she loves, she had her life shockingly altered forever in a vicious shark attack. She had to overcome the trauma of unexpectedly losing her arm. Real talk—most teenagers I know would be despondent for weeks if they unexpectedly lost their *cell phone* at the beach, much less their arm. Then, she had to navigate the sadness of potentially never enjoying the sport she loves so much. Once she got back into the water, she had to relearn how to balance on a surfboard with only one arm—and even if you've never stepped on a surfboard in your life, I'm sure you can appreciate the difficulty. After that, she had to summon the will to steadily climb up the surfing hierarchy to become one of the best surfers in the world. And, if you can imagine this, for every media interview, autograph signing, or speaking event, she'll likely be asked to recount the most traumatic day of her life, for the rest of her life. That's a lot, y'all.

I've never spoken to Bethany, but I'd be willing to bet that there's no chance that she would have accomplished any of her extraordinary accomplishments if she didn't accept her current circumstances. Or worse, if she constantly wished that fateful day didn't happen or that her arm would grow back—both of which are outside of her control. She said in an interview for *The Guardian* in 2020, "[T]o think that we are not going to have trouble sets ourselves up for mental struggles and the fact is we are all going to face hard times. When I lost my arm I was just thankful to be alive and that propelled me to have a more positive mindset."[20]

---

20 Graham Russell, "Bethany Hamilton: 'My fear of losing surfing was greater than my fear of sharks,'" March 6, 2020, https://www.theguardian.com/sport/2020/mar/07/bethany-hamilton-unstoppable-film-my-fear-of-losing-surfing-was-greater-than-my-fear-of-sharks.

If you mistake her quote as fluffy, saccharine sweet optimism or as toxic positivity, you're missing the point. This is hard-core resilience of the highest order. It's staring down an awful situation and saying, "This sucks … *and* I still have the agency to do something about it." In her case, it was living in gratitude and continuing to pursue her surfing dreams. This is the energy that we must wisely borrow as we work to create a more civil world. The world is a mess, and we can do something about it, unless we believe that we can't.

In chapter 2, one of the Shrug Squad's characteristics was that they felt that "someone else" will show up to do what's necessary to save the day. But, what if no one is coming? Despite a loving family who supported Bethany during the time before, during and after her shark attack, it was still up to her to fully own the things that were within her control:

Her actions.

Her effort.

Her attitude.

No one could do those things for her, and no one can do them for us either.

No, we can't fix our political dysfunction or bring peace to the Middle East by ourselves, but that doesn't give us the cover to do nothing because we feel that someone else will do it. The entropy facing the world cannot be healed by one person, but we can, and will, turn the tide if we can get enough people to step up to do what they can control.

Here's the formula:

1. Consistently lead by example with our actions, our effort, and our attitude to fight against entropy and do our part to create a more civil world.

2. Our actions, efforts, and attitudes will inspire another person, reinforce that person's faith in humanity, and encourage them to also take positive action.
3. Another person is added to the movement, and we're one step closer to uniting the world.

Complicate this if you choose, but that's really all there is to it. Whether it's finding peace at the Thanksgiving dinner table or finding peace in the Middle East, this is how it begins. It starts with the understanding that this work is our responsibility, and the good news is that we are in control. Or, we can sit back and wait for someone else to step up and do the right thing, just like Kitty Genovese's neighbors did.

If so, I can promise that our society will tragically face a similar fate that she did on that night.

Controlling the Controllables

As always, it's worth remembering that the hero in this story is the person staring back at us in the bathroom mirror. There is no one else who needs to take action more than you and I do. Embracing this sobering truth means to commit to controlling the controllables, and it simply requires asking yourself these simple questions:

Is There Action That I Can Take Right Now to Make This Situation Better?

This doesn't mean that your action will solve the problem or even that your action will make a significant difference. Ever since I was little, I had a habit of picking up litter whenever I saw it and putting it in a nearby trash can. This habit likely is not going to solve problematic toxic waste disposal practices that are harming our world as I'm writing this. But still, I have inarguably done two things: I handled what was within my capacity to change, and I made the world a better place through my actions. What if I didn't pick up the plastic six-pack holder, and it ended up in the ocean and strangled an innocent animal? Our actions don't need to end centuries of systemic racism, reverse global warming, or repair our divisive political climate by ourselves, but if there's something that's within our power to make these situations a *little bit* better, shouldn't we be doing it consistently? You and I have no idea how our seemingly small actions could positively affect someone.

Most important, we must reject the idea that just because we can't do everything, we shouldn't do something.

Am I Giving My Fullest Effort?

Effort is a subjective concept, but we always know when we're not giving everything that's within our power to give. Here's a concept that may be freeing: there are times when our best effort may not produce an objectively good result, and that is perfectly OK. For example, while writing this book that you're reading, there were many days when I could only string together two hundred words in a day. Some days I felt great, and I fired off two thousand words or more in a day. From a civility standpoint, there are days when I don't have the emotional capacity to engage in a difficult conversation. In those instances, if I asked myself, "Could I have done more?" many times, the answer would have been "no." On the flip side, if I'm being completely honest with myself, there are also times when I know that I could have put in more effort.

The key is to give your best effort as much as possible, and only you can be the judge of that. One thing is for sure, none of the challenges ahead of us will be fixed with half-assed energy.

Is My Attitude Helpful or Not?

Our attitude is our habitual way of thinking, and it is within our ability to control. One tactic that I have used to maintain proper perspective is the Six-and-Six Rule. It's simple—think of something that you are worried about right now (considering the state of the world as you're reading this, this shouldn't be too hard). Ask yourself, "Will this situation likely have a large impact on my life six months from now?" If the answer is "no," then don't give yourself any more than six minutes of your time to think about it.

One of the things that negatively impacts our attitude is that we give too much of our emotional energy to things that don't matter in the long term. Our energy is a precious—and finite—resource, and we cannot afford to waste an ounce of it as we do this work. If the situation you are worried about will likely be a big deal six months from now, then shift your focus to using whatever is within your control (namely, your actions, efforts, and attitudes) to improve it. If not, then allow yourself only six minutes to think about it before moving on with your day.

3. How to Address "Being Easily Influenced Not to Care"

Here's a sobering thought to chew on—for every problem that we're facing right now, we always have the capacity to make it worse. That's not meant to be depressing. In fact, I hope this is equal parts eye-opening and empowering. Armed with this information, why in the world would we ever consider doing anything that would knowingly make our problems worse?

The key word in that question is "knowingly." Most people don't consciously choose to do things that will make their lives harder, but that doesn't mean that they still don't do them. This is especially true when it comes to combating the third Shrug Squad characteristic that could trip us up as we work toward a more civil world: becoming easily influenced not to care.

To effectively address this, we must be hypervigilant about removing toxic influences from our lives. Here are two common, and potentially toxic, indulgences that if left unchecked will make us less resilient for the challenges ahead. Even more troubling, they can unwittingly harden our hearts, increase our animosity toward one another, and make our problems—and our capacity to deal with them—much worse.

Cable News

In their study, *Caught in a Dangerous World: Problematic News Consumption and Its Relationship to Mental and Physical Ill-Being*, researchers Bryan McLaughlin, Melissa Gotlieb, and Devin Mills shared some troubling data.

Bryan McLaughlin, one of the researchers for this study said:

"Witnessing these events unfold in the news can bring about a constant state of high alert in some people. This kicks their surveillance motives into overdrive and makes the world seem like a dark and dangerous place. For these individuals, a vicious cycle can develop in which, rather than tuning out, they become drawn further in. That is, obsessing over the news and checking for updates around the clock. This is in an effort to alleviate their emotional distress. However, this does not help. This is because, the more people check the news, the more other elements of their lives become disrupted as a result."[21]

According to their research, 73.6 percent of individuals recognized to have severe levels of problematic news consumption (when individuals frequently became so immersed and personally invested in news stories that the stories dominated the individual's waking thoughts, disrupted time with family and friends, made it difficult to focus on school or work, and contributed to restlessness and an inability to sleep) reported experiencing *mental ill-being* "quite a bit" or "very much," compared with only 8 percent of all other study participants. In addition, 61 percent of individuals with severe levels of problematic news reported experiencing *physical ill-being* "quite a bit" or "very much," compared with only 6.1 percent for all other study participants.[22]

If you know people who are problematic news watchers, I'm sure that these findings won't qualify as breaking news to you. Cable news is often called anger-tainment for a reason, so shoveling mounds of

---

21 Mark Peter, "Obsession with news affects physical health way more than you know," August 28, 2022, https://legitscience.com/obsession-with-news-affects-physical-health-way-more-than-expected/.

22 "News addiction linked to not only poor mental wellbeing but physical health too, new study shows," August 24, 2022, https://www.sciencedaily.com/releases/2022/08/220824102936.htm.

cortisol-spiking toxicity into our brains and overloading our sympathetic nervous symptoms for hours a day must negatively affect our mental and physical health in a significant way, no? While true, I don't believe that anyone who chooses to watch an extreme amount of news does so with the goal of accelerating their descent into mental illness. Similar to how smokers can confidently state that cigarettes help to lower their stress while ignoring the avalanche of detrimental aspects of that habit, hard-core news watchers can use the convenient, and also partially accurate, excuse that they are staying informed. However, this is a self-inflicted wound, because not only does compulsive news watching fail to solve any of our problems, but it also compounds those issues by making us less willing and able to address them in a meaningful way. It is very possible to stay actively informed on local and global news events without staring at a glowing blue box for hours on end, and I will give you a practical ICI later in this chapter on how you can do this.

I have a few chronic news watchers in my life, and I can say these things about them with confidence: they are not happy, and they have a skewed view of the world. The reason for this is because cable news taps into the evolutionary quirk in our brain known as the negativity bias, which states that when of equal intensity, negative stimuli will have a greater impact on one's psychological state than neutral or positive stimuli. Back in the prehistoric days, this bias kept our ancestors alive. Our ancestors had to assign more psychological energy to that one time when they almost got mauled by a saber-toothed tiger over the time when their caveman buddy gave them a compliment about their brilliant cave drawing. That additional mental energy is what kept them focused on credible threats to their lives and allowed the evolutionary lineage to continue to us. Unfortunately, for us in modern times, it's tough to behave civilly if we assign more emotional weight to the worst and most threatening aspects of our fellow humans, as opposed to the best.

In addition, I fear that excessive cable news watching does two other things that harm us. It divides us and desensitizes us. As mentioned, cable news producers are experts in exploiting the negativity bias in our brains to keep many of us hooked to the television. They must present a skewed view of a perceived threat (namely, the people from the "other side" whom the viewers perceive as the villains in their life stories) to keep viewers psychologically engaged, and it's working brilliantly—and at a severe cost to our ability to unite behind a more civil society.

If the news can make you believe that there are people lurking around every corner who are actively making the world less safe for you and your loved ones, taking money and resources from you, and lowering your overall quality of life, chances are that you're not going to consider being civil to them. Why would you? Cable news is brilliant at crafting a monolithic avatar of the enemy, and that makes them less complex and easier to hate. Adding the obvious nuance to the enemy—that they have families they love, they root for the same sports teams that you do, and that they surprisingly care about the same issues that you do—are inconvenient truths that restore their humanity, and the cable news stations have no interest in granting the enemy that courtesy anytime soon.

Worse than that though, it creates a convenient opening for bad faith leaders who happily exploit the monolithic avatar of the enemy to make viewers care less about others. If the Milgram experiment could successfully convince 65 percent of the study subjects to shock innocent people to death because an authority figure told them to do so, what could charismatic leaders convince their followers to do to the people whom they hate? If that thought doesn't scare you, it probably should.

Second, it desensitizes us. If you're old enough, do you remember how you responded to the news of the Columbine High School massacre in 1999 or the Sandy Hook Elementary School massacre in 2012? If you're anything like me, it probably broke you emotionally as you grappled to process the psychopathic evil of gunning down innocent children and educators who were simply going to school or doing their jobs. But these days? Many people hear a report of another mass shooting and, in true Shrug Squad fashion, respond with a half-hearted raise and lowering of their shoulders as if they heard a report of a cat stuck in a tree. This is not to say that people who become desensitized are bad people. But after mainlining a steady diet of senseless violence, terrorism, human suffering, bigotry, natural disasters, political misconduct, and wars abroad, our brains need to tap out from the deep emotional processing of these events to survive.

This desensitization, and the accompanying lack of empathy that is part of this package deal, makes it difficult to care deeply about our fellow humans.

Social Media

If a friend of yours needed a positive energy boost, or a practical way to improve their mental health or a means to regain their faith in the goodness of humanity, would your first recommendation be for them to go to their social media feed? Probably not.

So, isn't it a little weird that social media is the first place many people turn to when they want to take a rejuvenating (and, often ineffective) break from the world? The average person spends two hours and twenty-four minutes a day on social media. Mathematically speaking, on average, *that's 876 hours a year* when we are using a tool that is overwhelming us with negative energy, damaging our mental health, and making us less trusting of our fellow humans.

Don't take my word for it, though. Take a moment to consider the data. According to the statistics compiled by Bright Futures:

- 59 percent of adults who use social media report that it has impacted their mental health,
- 41 percent of women on social media report feeling pressure to present themselves in a certain way,
- 42 percent of people on social media report feeling more insecure about their appearance after using it,
- 37 percent of people on social media report being negatively impacted by political discussion on social media,
- 63 percent of people on social media report being lonely,
- 40 percent of people on social media report feeling anxious or depressed after using it,
- 60 percent of people on social media report feeling like they need to take a break from it, and
- 44 percent of people on social media report experiencing online harassment or abuse.[23]

Please don't mistake me for a curmudgeon who hates technological advances, baby animals, cloudless skies, and food that tastes good. Social media has a lot of wonderful aspects to it (I believe that my *Civil Unity* Facebook group is one of those wonderful places), but it is irresponsible to ignore the many addictive, harmful, and life-reducing aspects of it as well. Unfortunately, social media is known largely as

---

23 "70+ Social media and mental health statistics (2023)," https://www.brightfuturesny.com/post/social-media-and-mental-health-statistics.

a cesspool teeming with some of the most antisocial behaviors in existence—including bullying, stalking, body shaming, hate speech, and the spreading of misinformation and disinformation. Unlike cable news, anyone with a semi-functioning connected device, access to a decent Wi-Fi signal, and the ability to fog a mirror with their breath can spout an opinion online. And worst of all, it can be done under the cloak of anonymity.

Dealing with the folks who have questionable motives is only part of the challenge of social media. You will also have to combat the algorithms that ensure that the content that you interact with the most (which, unsurprisingly, is the content that aligns closest to your beliefs) will continue to faithfully appear in your feeds. There is nothing to be said about whether that information is accurate, reliable, or credible. It is one thing, though—*effective*. Specifically, at getting people to care less about their fellow humans, create and reinforce divisions, and harden hearts. If you don't believe me, as mentioned earlier, just wade into the comment section of any political social media post to see what I mean.

Removing Toxic Influences

Choosing to divest yourself from the news completely is not something that an engaged citizen should do, and I don't recommend it. Sticking our heads in the sand and pretending that horrific things aren't happening in the world solve nothing, and arguably, it exacerbates our problems. What we must do instead is behave thoughtfully about our news consumption. Here are a few practical suggestions for addressing the toxicity from both cable news and social media.

Cable News: Read Headlines Instead of Watching the News

Watching angry pundits and news anchors tell us for hours a day how our world is going to hell is not a recipe for mental wellness, peace of mind, and meaningful connection. And from an emotional standpoint, we tend to have a much more visceral response to watching the news rather than reading the news. Instead of watching three straight hours of prime-time cable news shows, go to your favorite reputable and credible news website, and pick one time during the day to scan the headlines. If you are so moved, allow yourself to click on one article per day. If you do that for a week, you will likely be just as informed as you were when you were watching hours of news, without the constant stream of cortisol flowing through your veins.

Cable News: Turn Off News Alerts

If you're a problematic news watcher, the last thing that you need is breaking news alerts hitting your smartphone multiple times a day. That is like an alcoholic being reminded multiple times a day that he has a flask of whiskey in his pocket. Most of the news alerts that are hitting your phone aren't truly "breaking news," and if something earth-shattering is happening in the world, please trust that you will know about it around the same time that everyone else does.

Cable News: Temporary Detox

As mentioned, unplugging permanently from the news probably isn't possible or recommended. But once a month, can you commit to going a week without consuming any news of any kind? This means for one week, there will be no watching news, no scanning headlines on your favorite news website, *literally nothing*. When the urge strikes, take a walk, and listen to an uplifting podcast or audiobook. The goal is to show your brain that you are in charge of your news consumption instead of the other way around.

Similar to cable news watching, we must be thoughtful about our social media consumption. Here are some ideas to incorporate.

Social Media: Fountain versus Drain

Think of the people on your social media feed right now, and ask yourself this very important question: "Does this person fill me up and nourish me like a fountain, or do they drain me?" View your social media feed like it's the living room in your home. If you came home from a long day at work, and you saw an acquaintance of yours (not even an actual friend!) putting her nasty muddy shoes on your dining room table, leaving fast-food grease stains on your clean couch, and blasting Limp Bizkit's *Greatest Hits* album from your Bluetooth speaker on top volume, I'm assuming you would immediately throw this person out of your home. Shouldn't the same apply to your feed? If someone you barely know is coming into your home and draining you by bringing mindless stress and drama to your feed, block them unapologetically.

Social Media: Keep Your Cell Phone Out of Your Bedroom

A lot of people surf on social media until they drift off to sleep, and then upon waking, they resume their social media addiction. One way to overcome this is to stop sleeping with your cell phone in your bedroom. If you use your cell phone as your alarm clock, I'm urging you to buy a dedicated alarm clock—the cost is worth the mental health benefits. Get in the habit of starting and ending your days intentionally instead of bookending your days with unproductive social media arguments, FOMO (for the uninitiated, that is the "Fear of Missing Out"), toxic anger, and political drama. Not to mention, going to bed watching the news or scrolling through social media will not only wreak havoc on the quality of your sleep, but it will also likely impact your mood the following day. And please trust that few things will be more important as we engage in this work than managing our mood and getting a good night's sleep.

Social Media: Delete the Social Media Apps from Your Phone

If you are particularly serious about maintaining your mental health, consider deleting the social media apps from your smartphone. All of your friends and connections won't disappear, and they can still be accessed through your web browser, if necessary. The best part is that doing so will drastically reduce the amount of time of mindlessly surfing on social media.

Emotional Regulation

I saved the hardest and, most important point, in this chapter for last. Everything in this chapter up to this point is meaningless if we are not able to effectively regulate our emotions. I already laid out many of the challenges waiting for you. Difficult colleagues and bosses, hateful exes, rude and inconsiderate neighbors, social media trolls, and cable news anchors slamming you with unceasing bad news, to name a few. Needless to say, if we leave our emotional well-being in the hands of these people, we're screwed.

The practice of emotional regulation is arguably one of the most important skills to master in creating a more civil world, and this is going to require constant vigilance and effort. Failing to do this means that we could find ourselves spending our free time devising clever clapbacks to social media bots in the comment section of political posts, keying your ex's car when you see it in the grocery store parking lot, pummeling the guy behind you in line because he accidentally stepped on the back of your new Jordans, or cursing out your aunt in front of your kids because you found out that she's voting for the candidate whom you hate.

Committing to the hardest aspects of this work means that we can't allow ourselves to consistently succumb to our least helpful emotional impulses. Emotional regulation, however, ensures that we will stay focused on what matters without losing control, we will handle conflict effectively, and we will serve as a role model for positive communication. And this cannot be said enough—all of this can be done while fighting like hell for the causes that you believe in.

If you're ready, let's start with three simple ideas that can serve us.

Know Your Triggers

Unless you have reached a level of inner peace where nothing in this world makes you angry, frustrated, or annoyed (and if you did somehow figure this out, can you kindly send me an email and teach me your ways, please?), chances are you've been emotionally triggered or activated by something or someone. The intentional exercise of knowing your emotional triggers can go a long way in reducing their power over your emotional state once you inevitably encounter them.

An emotional trigger is something (a person, a situation, a place, an object, a smell, a sound, or something else) that prompts a strong emotional reaction. Emotional triggers don't have to be related to deeply traumatic episodes. It could be as simple as a reminder of an unpleasant memory that serves as a trigger for you. If you had to give an important presentation in front of the executive team and you completely bombed, you may be triggered whenever you walk past the boardroom, when you see the CEO, or whenever you have to present in front of people in the future.

Personally speaking, I have an extremely long list of emotional triggers, but for brevity's sake, here are my top five when it comes to civility:

- people who are terrible listeners
- people who deny the existence of intolerance (e.g., racism, homophobia, Islamophobia, or anti-Semitism)
- people who are rude, or behave in an entitled manner, toward service professionals (restaurant servers, flight attendants, retail employees, or call center representatives)
- people who abuse animals
- people who make fun of people with physical or mental disabilities

Depending on the severity of the situation, my emotional responses to these situations range from intense anger to exasperation to sadness. Thankfully, by engaging in the exercise of noting what truly gets under my skin, I'm more prepared to *not* get emotionally hijacked whenever I encounter one of my top five triggers.

There are three steps to this. First, list out your top three to five civility triggers (particularly, the things that elicit an emotional response, specific to how we treat one another). The more detailed you can be in this exercise, the better.

Second, describe in detail how it makes you feel, emotionally *and* physically. For example, when I see a dog trapped inside of a sweltering hot car in the brutal summer months, while its human is inside of an air-conditioned shopping mall, I feel an anger that borders on rage. In addition, I experience a feeling in the pit of my stomach that presents in a similar manner to nausea. Because I'm familiar with these feelings, it is my cue that I will lose control if I don't get myself in check, quickly (more on how to do that, momentarily).

Third, try to understand why these situations are so emotionally charged for you. On my trigger list, the terrible listener trigger may seem out of place compared with the others. So, why does that bother me so much? Remember the "Pee-Gate" story that I shared in chapter 1? I held (and, apparently, still hold) some strong anger toward my teacher for ignoring me and not listening to me when I said that I really needed to use the restroom. My brain made a strong association that people who don't listen to others can cause a great deal of harm. To this day, I don't trust or feel emotionally safe around people who are poor listeners.

Once we have our triggers sorted out, we can move to the second part of emotional regulation.

Calm Is Strong

One of my good buddies would always say, "There are two types of people in a crisis. The ones who always need to be calmed down, and the ones who always calm others down." While I know that most phrases that begin with "There are two types of people …" can be a little cringey (not to mention, largely untrue), this one is worth thinking about. When things go wrong, are you the type of person who needs to be calmed down, or do you calm others down?

It's fascinating to me that in *literal* life-or-death situations, like someone choking on a piece of food in a restaurant or a patient's heart unexpectedly stopping in the hospital, it's always calm and quick thinking that saves lives. When someone is choking, there are minutes (potentially, less) for someone to administer cardiopulmonary resuscitation (CPR) and dislodge the food from the person's airway. If the CPR practitioner spent the first ninety seconds running around the restaurant with her arms flailing over her head like one of those weird inflatable people who are outside of car dealerships, the person would suffocate and die. While freaking out seems like a reasonable response given the stress of a life-or-death situation, for whatever reason, when a crisis hits, some people can lock in and remain calm.

If they are able to do it, shouldn't we be able to tap into the same power when we're dealing with the stress of an emotionally triggering moment that's *not* life or death? Return to your trigger list for a moment. When you experienced something that triggered you, did you respond in a way that you're not proud of? If so, we need a strategy.

The first thing you can do in the moment when you're triggered (remember, at this point, you should know what your triggers feel like, physically) is to intentionally use breathing exercises to activate the body's natural relaxation response. One incredibly effective way to do this is to breathe deeply from your diaphragm, often known as diaphragmatic breathing or belly breathing. Most people typically breathe from their chest, but if you are engaging in belly breathing, your belly should fully extend as you slowly inhale through your nose and retract as you slowly breathe out through your mouth. As you belly breathe, your chest should stay still. To ensure that you are doing this correctly, you can place one hand on your belly as it expands and your other hand on your chest to make sure that it is not moving as you breathe. Belly breathing is a simple, but effective, way to lower your heart rate and blood pressure, interrupt the emotional wave that's about to consume you, and send a clear signal to your conscious brain that you're OK and you're still in control. In addition, another powerful breathing technique to reduce stress and calm your nervous system is to practice daily box breathing. The box breathing process is simple: slowly inhale for four seconds, then hold your breath for four seconds, then slowly exhale for four seconds, and then finally hold for four seconds. You can repeat this four-step box process as often as necessary. The beauty of both belly breathing and box breathing is that they can be done pretty much anywhere or at any time when you need to feel more relaxed and in control.

Second, choose a mantra that you can silently say to yourself when you're triggered. My mantra is "calm is strong," and I've used it for years when I've been triggered. There's something powerful about focusing on a short phrase ("calm is strong" or "you got this"), or one calming word ("chill" or "relax") also has the power of interrupting the wave of stress and anger and sending the signal to your brain that you can handle what's coming next.

This tactic is not an easy one, and practice makes perfect, so please don't be discouraged if you don't master this immediately.

Cognitive Reframing

The late author Dr. Wayne Dyer once said, "If you change the way you look at things, the things you look at change." This quote changed my life and introduced me to the idea of cognitive reframing.

Cognitive reframing is the process of changing how people, situations, or events are viewed in a way that better serves us. Savvy customer service representatives do this consistently after putting a customer on hold for an extended period of time. Upon resuming the call, there is a significant difference between the customer service representative saying, "Thank you so much for your patience," versus saying, "I'm so sorry for keeping you waiting." In both cases, the hold time was the same, but reframing the unpleasant experience of being on hold as something positive (being thanked for your patience) instead of something negative (reminding you of how long you've been waiting) can change how we view a situation.

Can we do something similar when we're triggered? The key is often to remain curious and reject immediate judgment. If someone was rude to me, I could judge them as a terrible human being and be done with it. However, it is a more challenging practice to remain in curiosity and possibly think, "Maybe she's in a hurry or maybe she's managing a lot of stress in her life." To be clear, this is not a way to excuse bad behavior. It's a way to view situations in a different way that better serves us, potentially find common ground, and possibly acknowledge that we might have acted in a similar way if faced with the same circumstances.

One thing to be aware of is the unfortunate mutated version of cognitive reframing known as toxic positivity, when people refuse to acknowledge any less-than-joyful feelings and emotions, and they force happy thoughts on deeply unpleasant situations. For example, if you just discovered your spouse has been having a year-long affair behind your back, the last thing that you'd want to hear is something like, "On the bright side, at least now you know that he never loved you. Now you're free to find someone who does!" This doesn't fall into the category of cognitive reframing; it falls into the category of appearing clueless and unable to read a room.

Sometimes, we need to sit with our feelings, grieve and process them without being forced into a state of positivity. Cognitive reframing, on the contrary, is about being open-minded, curious, and seeing if there's another way to process the situation that happened to us.

Preparing for the Outer Work

Some people are so fired up to begin the outer work of civility that they end up forgetting about the inner work of civility. Almost always, those are the ones, while well-intentioned, who end up burning out first. Ignoring the importance of rest, renewal, and mental wellness on this civility journey is like going on a long road trip and declaring, "I'm too busy driving to stop and get gas!" We both know how that story will end. Please don't make the mistake of jumping into the complex work that's to come in the following chapters without pausing to put the ICIs at the end of this chapter to work, first.

The world needs you to be energized because it's only going to get more challenging from here. But if you've handled the inner work, there's no doubt that you'll be ready for the outer work—and when you're ready, that outer work begins next.

INTENTIONAL CONSISTENT INTERVENTION #2: *TOUGH LOVE SELF-CARE*

From the following bulleted list, choose one item from the Tough Love Self-Care list (not two, not four—*just one*) that you are committing to actively improve for thirty straight days:

- managing healthy boundaries (saying "No")
- removing yourself from toxic relationships
- prioritizing rest and fully unplugging while on vacation
- making healthy choices and/or exercising
- forgiving others (and yourself, if necessary)
- asking for help and/or reaching out to a therapist

ICI Steps:

1. In your *Civil Unity Journal* at the beginning of each day for thirty straight days, write down the specific actions you are committing to take in pursuit of your selected Tough Love Self-Care goal. It is fine if you repeat the same actions over the thirty-day period.
2. At the end of each day, record your successes in your *Civil Unity Journal* (what went well and why) and your opportunities for improvement (what didn't go well and why).
3. At the end of the thirty-day period, reflect on your overall success in achieving your selected Tough Love Self-Care goal. If you feel like you have more work to do in this area, continue this process for another thirty

days. If you are feeling like you have this area of your life under control, select another Tough Love Self-Care goal, and begin the aforementioned ICI steps for thirty straight days.

INTENTIONAL CONSISTENT INTERVENTION #3: *REINFORCE OR RECRUIT YOUR CREW*

The three types of people who you want to have in your crew are someone who will feel with you, who will laugh with you, and who will stand with you.

ICI Steps:

1. Take inventory of your inner circle. Ask yourself, "Do I have people in my inner circle who will feel with me, laugh with me, and stand with me?" If so, in your *Civil Unity Journal*, write the person's (or, peoples') name(s) who satisfies each category. For example, Christine is a person who will feel with me, Kris will laugh with me, and James will stand with me.
2. After you have identified the people in your life who meet the criteria, intentionally reinforce those relationships. As often as possible, but at least once a week, connect meaningfully by grabbing a bite to eat together, hopping on a call, exchanging texts, going on a walk or a hike—anything that continues to strengthen your relationship, do it. In your *Civil Unity Journal*, write down the specific ways that you plan to reinforce your relationship with the people who will feel with you, laugh with you, and stand with you.

3. If you don't have people who meet the criteria, then work on recruiting them into your life. In your *Civil Unity Journal*:
   - Write down your top three interests (in my case, civility, basketball, and self-improvement), and then search for local or online affinity groups for your identified interests. Commit to joining one affinity group in any of your identified interests, and stay open to meeting new people and making meaningful connections.
   - Write down a way that you will volunteer your time, and determine a realistic time frame for you to do so (e.g., "I will volunteer at the nearby swim school, once a week"). As mentioned earlier, while volunteering, stay open to meeting new people and making meaningful connections.
   - Write down a way that you will stay the course if or when it becomes challenging to find meaningful connections. For example, searching for a different affinity group and/or volunteer opportunity that better suits you. Remember, you can always join the *Civil Unity* Facebook group as a great place to make new connections with others.

INTENTIONAL CONSISTENT INTERVENTION #4: *THE SIX-AND-SIX RULE AND THE CONTROL QUESTIONS*

The only things that we have complete control over in our lives are our actions, our efforts, and our attitudes. Whenever we get caught up in circumstances that fall outside of our control, apply the Six-and-Six Rule, and consistently ask the following control questions to refocus on our agency to impact the circumstances within our control:

ICI Steps:

1. Think of a situation in your life right now that is worrisome to you or is causing you stress. Write it down in your *Civil Unity Journal*.
2. Apply the Six-and-Six Rule to the situation that you documented in step 1 of this ICI by asking yourself, "Will this situation likely have a large impact on my life six months from now?"
3. If your answer is "yes," then document in your *Civil Unity Journal* what you can specifically do that is within your control (namely, your actions, your efforts, and your attitudes) to address it by answering the control questions:
    - "Is there action I can take right now to make this situation better? What are those specific actions?"
    - "Am I giving my fullest effort in addressing this situation? Why or why not? If not, what do I need to change so that I can consistently give more effort?"
    - "Is my attitude in regard to this situation helpful or not? Why or why not? If not, what action can I take to improve my attitude?"
4. If your answer is "no" to the question in step 2 of this ICI, then don't give yourself any more than six minutes of your time to think about it.

INTENTIONAL CONSISTENT INTERVENTION #5: *SCAN HEADLINES*

Instead of watching hours of cable news, choose to scan headlines from a news website instead.

ICI Steps:

1. For one week every month, stop watching cable news.
2. During that week, scan headlines from your favorite news website, and allow yourself to click on one article per day.
3. In your *Civil Unity Journal*, write how you will use your newfound free time to do something uplifting for yourself or for a loved one.
4. After the week is over, ask yourself, "Do I feel as informed about current events as I was last week? Do I feel better (physically, mentally, or emotionally) after avoiding cable news programming for a week? Why or why not?" Record your responses in your *Civil Unity Journal*.
5. Repeat the process next month.

INTENTIONAL CONSISTENT INTERVENTION #6: *BREAK THE CYCLE*

Break the cycle of being inundated with breaking news alerts by turning off all news alerts that are pushed to any of your connected devices.

ICI Steps:

1. Identify the connected devices that are receiving push news alerts (your smartphone, smartwatch, tablet, or computer).

2. Turn off all alerts for a week.
3. After the week is over, ask yourself, "Do I feel as informed about current events as I was last week? Am I willing to keep the news alerts off of my devices for another week? Why or why not?" Record your responses in your *Civil Unity Journal*.

INTENTIONAL CONSISTENT INTERVENTION #7: *THE SEVEN-DAY DETOX*

Commit to temporarily detox yourself from the news by not intentionally consuming any news on television or on the internet for one week.

ICI Steps:

1. For one week every month, stop consuming news of any kind.
2. After the week is over, ask yourself, "Do I feel as informed about current events as I was last week? Do I feel better (physically, mentally, or emotionally) after avoiding all news content for a week? Why or why not?"
3. Record your responses in your *Civil Unity Journal*.

INTENTIONAL CONSISTENT INTERVENTION #8: *FOUNTAIN VERSUS DRAIN*

Take inventory of the people whom you follow on social media and determine if they figuratively fill you up like a fountain or drain you.

ICI Steps:

1. Identify the people whom you are connected to, or follow, on social media whose content and posts encourage you to critically think, add value to your life, or uplift your mood. These are the people who "fill you up" like a fountain. Write their names down in your *Civil Unity Journal*.
2. Identify the people whom you are connected to, or follow, on social media whose content and posts are drama filled, annoying, or hateful. These are the people who drain you. Write their names down in your *Civil Unity Journal* (pro-tip: use a pseudonym if you think your journal could ever end up in the wrong hands).
3. Block or remove the people from your "Drain" list from your social media feed.
4. Repeat this process on a monthly basis.

INTENTIONAL CONSISTENT INTERVENTION #9: *NO PHONE ZONE*

Keep cell phone usage to a minimum before going to bed and upon waking, and commit to no cell phone usage in bed.

ICI Steps:

1. Do not use your cell phone in bed or go to sleep with your cell phone next to your bed for one week (side note: if you have a job where you are on call, this understandably may not be possible).

2. If you use your cell phone as your alarm clock, if possible, invest in a dedicated alarm clock. If that is not possible, keep your cell phone on the other side of the room so that you will be forced to get out of bed to turn off your alarm.
3. During this week, do not look at your cell phone for thirty minutes before going to bed *and* for thirty minutes after waking up.
4. After the week is over, record in your *Civil Unity Journal* any positive outcomes (e.g., improved sleep) or negative outcomes (heightened anxiety).
5. Repeat this process once a month.

INTENTIONAL CONSISTENT INTERVENTION #10: *BECOME ANTISOCIAL*

No, this isn't about literally becoming antisocial (or even being anti-social media). This ICI is about experiencing what it feels like not to have social media notifications pinging your cell phone constantly.

ICI Steps:

1. Turn off the social media notifications on all of your connected devices for one week. You are still free to log in to your social media accounts using an internet browser, if you choose.
2. At the end of the week, use your cell phone's screen time app to compare your social media usage to the previous week's usage when the social media apps

were still on your phone. Was there a difference? Record the answer in your *Civil Unity Journal*.

3. Repeat this process on a monthly basis.

INTENTIONAL CONSISTENT INTERVENTION #11: *KNOW YOUR TRIGGERS*

Become more aware of your emotional triggers.

ICI Steps:

1. In your *Civil Unity Journal*, list your top three civility triggers (specifically, the behaviors of others that evoke an emotional response from you).
2. Describe in your *Civil Unity Journal* how your triggers make you feel emotionally and physically.
3. Describe in your *Civil Unity Journal* why these triggers are so emotionally charged for you.
4. Repeat this process once a month.

INTENTIONAL CONSISTENT INTERVENTION #12: *BREATHE AND SPEAK*

Practice breathing techniques and empowering self-talk to maintain emotional regulation.

ICI Steps:

1. Practice breathing deeply from your diaphragm whenever you are feeling an acute stress response because of being emotionally triggered. To do this effectively, put one hand over your chest to ensure that it stays still as you breathe, and put your other hand over

your belly to ensure that it expands as you breathe. Specifically, slowly inhale through your nose as your belly expands, and then slowly exhale through your mouth as your belly contracts. This is a powerfully effective way to initiate the body's natural relaxation response.

2. On a daily basis, practice box breathing to reduce stress and calm your nervous system. Inhale slowly for four seconds, then hold your breath for four seconds, then exhale slowly for four seconds, and finally hold your breath for four seconds. Repeat this process as often as needed. In your *Civil Unity Journal*, write down the dedicated time(s) of day when you will practice box breathing (e.g., upon waking, on your commute to work, before meals, while taking a walk, or in the shower).
3. Develop a short self-talk mantra that you can say to yourself whenever you're triggered. For example, my mantra is "calm is strong." Write your self-talk mantra in your *Civil Unity Journal*, and use it as often as necessary.

INTENTIONAL CONSISTENT INTERVENTION #13: *REFRAME*

Reframe how people, situations, or events are viewed in a way that better serves you.

ICI Steps:

1. Whenever you witness a person behaving in a way that you don't understand, ask yourself from a place of curiosity, "Is there anything about this situation that I may not understand?"

2. If the answer to the previous question is "yes," attempt to reframe the situation and view it from a slightly different perspective.
3. In your *Civil Unity Journal*, write down your initial perceptions of the situation, and then how you reframed it to better serve you.

CHAPTER 5
Defeating Misinformation and Disinformation

The crisis we face about truth and reliable facts is predicated less on the ability to get people to believe the wrong thing as it is on the ability to get people to doubt the right thing.

—JAMAIS CASCIO

Chances are that you know that most humans only use 10 percent of their brains, if you swallow chewing gum it will remain in your stomach undigested for seven years, constantly cracking your knuckles will give you arthritis, and sugar makes children annoyingly hyperactive.

Except, none of those statements are true.[24] So, then why do so many people believe them?

These myths are easily believed, because they seem plausible at a quick glance. And unless you are willing to stress test these myths against some intellectual rigor, it's probably easier to accept them as fact and move on to more important matters, which is fine if we're talking about undigested chewing gum and arthritic hands, but it's a dangerous strategy to apply as the default mode for processing information.

Unfortunately for us, the more advanced forms of untruths, known as misinformation and disinformation, are not only dangerous, but they also play a significant role in eroding civil discourse in our society. While these terms are often used interchangeably, misinformation and disinformation are only similar in the sense that both are false or inaccurate. Misinformation is when false information is spread without the intent to harm or deceive others. Disinformation, on the contrary, is about intentionally spreading false or misleading information, often for political, social, or economic gain. When people believe information that is factually inaccurate, it can accelerate the erosion of trust in our fellow humans, deepen existing divisions in society, amplify unproductive disagreements, and inspire fear, hate, and violence—all of which makes it much harder to live in a civil world.

Case in point—according to a 2020 NPR/Ipsos poll, 17 percent of Americans believed that a group of Satan-worshipping elites who run a child sex ring are trying to control our politics and media.

---

24 BEST LIFE EDITORS, "50 Well-known "facts" that are actually just common myths," JUNE 12, 2020, https://bestlifeonline.com/common-myths/.

Equally as alarming, in the same poll, an additional 37 percent of Americans said that they *didn't know* if it was true.[25] So basically, over half of Americans either believe that a group of anti-Christ-loving pedophiles is secretly controlling America or they're basically like "Eh … it sounds like it could happen." This may be great news if you're looking to find the next target to fall for your shell game scam outside of a busy tourist spot, but for the rest of us, this is very problematic or potentially fatal.

A twenty-eight-year-old man named Edgar Maddison Welch presumably was one of the 17 percent of Americans mentioned in the previous paragraph who believed in this baseless conspiracy theory. Once he heard that the Comet Ping Pong pizzeria in Washington, DC, was serving as a hideout for a child sex trafficking ring, on December 4, 2016, he made the nearly five-hour drive from his home in North Carolina to the nation's capital armed with an AR-15 semiautomatic rifle, a .38 handgun, and a folding knife with the intentions of rescuing child victims who didn't exist.

This was the frightening culmination of the fake news story known as "Pizzagate," which pushed the false idea that Comet Ping Pong was the secret headquarters for a pedophile ring. The believers began by harassing the pizzeria's owner and staff online with protests and death threats and ended with Mr. Welch firing his weapon inside of the pizzeria, which led to his subsequent arrest and conviction. Thankfully, no one was injured or killed, but it's clear that this situation could have ended very differently.

That's what's so horrifying about all of this. The idea that people could easily and willingly believe demonstrably false information

25 Joel Rose, "Even if it's 'bonkers,' poll finds many believe QAnon and other conspiracy theories," December 30, 2020, https://www.npr.org/2020/12/30/951095644/even-if-its-bonkers-poll-finds-many-believe-qanon-and-other-conspiracy-theories.

could have severe implications for the future of our world. Everything including our day-to-day safety, our public health, how we educate our children, the outcomes of elections, and the future viability of our environment and our democracy could be influenced negatively by people believing in lies, at scale. If you don't think that there are some very sophisticated minds with equally impure intentions who are working feverishly to exploit this vulnerability to reach their nefarious ends, can you please send me your cell number so that I can sell you an extended auto warranty that you don't need?

None of this is particularly funny, so I'm not sure why I'm cracking dumb jokes when the future of our world is at stake. What in the heck can we do about this?

Critical Thinking and Intellectual Humility

To effectively defeat misinformation and disinformation, and improve our civil discourse in the world, we must commit to two things: critical thinking and intellectual humility—committing in the sense that we must practice, model, and live these two enhanced thinking skills consistently—and we have to help as many people as possible to do the same.

Critical Thinking

Critical thinking in its simplest definition is the ability to effectively analyze information to form a well-reasoned judgment—or, in other words, it's thinking about our thinking. That sounds simple, but when done well, it's a complex intellectual skill. Our ticket for entry requires us to engage in a few behaviors, at minimum: actively and objectively evaluate information, question our assumptions, examine different perspectives, and apply logic to reach conclusions that are based on credible evidence, instead of our opinions, our feelings, or personal biases. If that sounds like a lot of hard work, you would be right. Unfortunately, that's why most people don't do it. Considering the current stakes, we can't afford to be like most people.

We are drowning in information—whether the source is from cable news outlets, our social media echo chambers, our colleagues, our friends, and even our weird uncle whom we only see during the holidays. It would be naïve to believe that all the information that we consume from these sources is trustworthy and credible, and that's what makes habitually accepting information at face value such a dangerous bet. To build a more civil world, the willingness and the ability to pause, become fiercely curious, and examine the accuracy of the evidence and the quality of the source to arrive at reasoned decisions and judgments is more important than ever.

Similar to playing the piano, speaking a foreign language, or actively applying civility in our lives, critical thinking requires dedicated practice. Educational psychologists Linda Elder and Richard Paul developed a theory of stages of development in critical thinking that we can move through in our lives:

1. The "Unreflective Thinker" is largely unaware of the importance of critical thinking in all facets of life and doesn't consistently practice any critical thinking methods.
2. The "Challenged Thinker" is enlightened, having been made aware of the importance of critical thinking and of their own lack of critical thinking skills.

3. The "Beginning Thinker" has committed to making critical thinking a part of their life and has begun to self-monitor and observe their own thinking practices and habits.
4. The "Practicing Thinker" understands what types of changes they must make to their "old" patterns of thinking and are committed to actively practicing critical thinking.
5. The "Advanced Thinker" has established excellent critical thinking habits and is beginning to reap the benefits of applying these habits throughout their lives.[26]

While it would be lovely if everyone could jump to the Advanced Thinker stage, for the sake of creating a more civil world, I don't want to get too greedy about this. I believe that the world would dramatically change overnight if more people simply jumped from Stage One to Stage Two, and that's all I'm shooting for.

Intellectual Humility

Poet and novelist Charles Bukowski once said, "The problem with the world is that the intelligent people are full of doubts, while the stupid ones are full of confidence." While it may be tempting to label some people as stupid (especially the ones who don't agree with us), my hope is that *everyone*—whether you think that they are smart, stupid, or in between—will become less confident in their beliefs.

Intellectual humility in its simplest form is the acknowledgment that our knowledge about an idea or topic is incomplete and that our beliefs may be incorrect. Being intellectually humble doesn't mean

26 "Developing critical thinking skills," February 16, 2023, https://www.thinkinghabitats.com/blog/developing-critical-thinking-skills.

that our beliefs will weakly fold like a lawn chair in a hurricane at the first sign of challenge. It means that we are aware that we could be wrong, we acknowledge our blind spots, we become seekers of information instead of validation, and most of all, we have released the ego-fueled need to be right.

The opposites of intellectual humility are arrogance and closed-mindedness—neither of which will serve us in creating a more civil world. Intellectually humble people tend to be deeply curious, more open to hearing and considering other people's viewpoints, and willing to evaluate new information and, if warranted, admit they are wrong and update their beliefs.

Do you know anyone like this? I do, and I can confidently say that they are some of the most refreshing people to be around. Even if you don't know of anyone who is intellectually humble, I'm sure that we can agree that arrogant and closed-minded people are the least enjoyable people to share space with. But enough about everyone else, let's bring this back to you. Are you intellectually humble?

Researchers at Duke University developed a tool known as the *General Intellectual Humility Scale* where people rated how closely each of the following statements describes them on a five-point scale ranging from "not at all like me" to "very much like me":

- I question my own opinions, positions, and viewpoints because they could be wrong.
- I reconsider my opinions when presented with new evidence.
- I recognize the value in opinions that are different from my own.
- I accept that my beliefs and attitudes may be wrong.
- In the face of conflicting evidence, I am open to changing my opinions.

- I like finding out new information that differs from what I already think is true.[27]

Hopefully, you evaluated yourself honestly after reviewing the statements from the *General Intellectual Humility Scale*, and if you feel like there's more work for you to do, please begin the process today. Even if you walk away from this section with a little less confidence in your beliefs and with a renewed interest in questioning your opinions, that would be a fabulous start.

A word of caution, though. At this point, you may be thinking, "This is great and all, but what about my neighbor Greg? He hasn't had a critical thought in his life, and he's the least intellectually humble person on earth. Why do I need to critically think and be intellectually humble, when he doesn't?" Two things—first, we'll deal with Greg and people like him in the final four chapters, so hang tight. Second, and more important, Greg isn't the person who is going to unite the world. *It's going to be people like you.* As frustrating as people like he can be, we need to focus on what we have the power to control, namely, ensuring that our house is in order.

Arguably, critical thinking and intellectual humility are the two most important ICIs to slow the entropy of incivility. Both ensure that we will become better equipped to thoughtfully examine information, less willing to be driven by our ego-based urges to be right, and most of all, that we are less susceptible to manipulation, all of which will be needed when engaging with the fraternal twins of deception: misinformation and disinformation.

27 Mark Leary, "What does intellectual humility look like?" November 3, 2021, https://greatergood.berkeley.edu/article/item/what_does_intellectual_humility_look_like.

The Speed of Deception

Mark Twain once said, "A lie can travel halfway around the world while the truth is putting on its shoes." The wisdom in this quote is why misinformation and disinformation are such formidable adversaries in the battle for a more civil world. As of 2022, the global smartphone penetration rate was estimated at 68 percent.[28] Pause on that number for a moment. That could mean that roughly 5.2 billion people across our world have access to a relatively user-friendly supercomputer in their pocket. This powerful computing device can connect us to an infinite amount of information, in mere seconds. While that can be a wonderful thing, it also means that it is now easier than ever for anyone to spread false information to any corner of the earth quickly.

For example, let's say that one of your social media contacts shares a false story from a news outlet that a well-known actor was busted for masterminding an elaborate Ponzi scheme from the basement of his home. Perhaps the news outlet acted too swiftly in hopes of being the ones to break the story first, and they didn't have their facts in order before reporting it. Arguably, there was no ill intent, but it doesn't lessen the potential damage that is done by sharing this false story publicly. The damage is exacerbated when your social media buddy decides to share that story (it's from a news source, so it must be credible, right?), then you read it, decide that it's credible too because you trust your friend, and share it on your social network. This is how misinformation spreads, and like Mr. Twain said, it's already halfway around the world. Even if the news outlet decides to figuratively put on its shoes and offer a retraction, the damage has been done, and fewer people will likely share the retraction than the sensationalized false story.

---

28 https://www.statista.com/statistics/203734/global-smartphone-penetration-per-capita-since-2005/.

The Pizzagate scandal is a powerful example of the power of misinformation. Many of the people who were spreading this story weren't doing so to deceive anyone—they actually believed this story was the truth. More than that, because they rightly believed so deeply in how morally reprehensible child sex rings are, they felt obligated to do something about it. While Mr. Welch was driving to Washington, DC, on that fateful day, he recorded a selfie video in his car for his young daughters who were at home in which he said, "I can't let you grow up in a world that's so corrupt by evil without at least standing up for you and for the other children just like you."

His heart might have been in the right place, but unfortunately, the siren song of misinformation ensured that his brain and the rest of his body were not.[29]

As bad as that is, disinformation is far more nefarious because it is intentionally designed to deceive. Let's say you happen to live in a swing state, and Election Day is a few weeks away. The pre-election polls are predicting that it's going to be a very close race in your state between Candidate A and Candidate B. A shady operative of Candidate A could start spreading a false story saying that because of the anticipated record voter turnout for this election, and in hopes of lessening wait times at poll locations, voters who support Candidate A will vote on Tuesday (Election Day) and the voters who support Candidate B will vote the following day on Wednesday. This is a sophomoric form of disinformation for sure, but in a swing state where the margin of victory could come down to less than a percentage point, this could convince *just enough* people to stay at home on Election Day (who wants to wait in long lines, right?) and deliver victory to Candidate A.

---

29 Michael E. Miller, "Pizzagate's violent legacy," https://www.washingtonpost.com/dc-md-va/2021/02/16/pizzagate-qanon-capitol-attack/.

A real-life example of disinformation that I'm very familiar with is the following graphic:

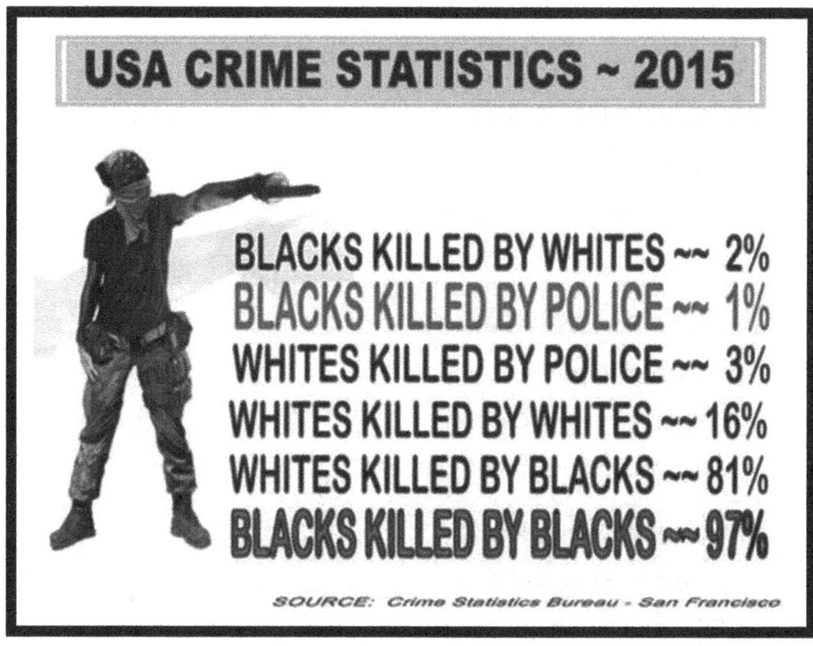

This image went viral in 2015 when prominent politicians and influencers shared this freely on their social media channels. The problem is that the statistics in the graphic are bogus and have been debunked by numerous independent fact-checking websites like factcheck.org and politifact.com, which granted this graphic its infamous "pants on fire" rating.

Still though, did we really need to call in the fact-checkers for this one? Just a simple Google search would show that the source of this graphic "Crime Statistics Bureau—San Francisco" doesn't exist. Unfortunately, the creator of this graphic wisely knew that if they had (1) an image of a stereotypical Black criminal in a bandanna pointing a gun, (2) statistics that reinforced deeply held beliefs and biases, (3) a credible-sounding source authoring the data, and (4) a person of authority sharing it, then this graphic would spread like wildfire without anyone pausing to examine its accuracy before sharing it. That assumption was spot on.

For the record, here are the accurate statistics from a real source, the Federal Bureau of Investigation (FBI):

Blacks killed by Blacks

- Graphic: 97 percent
- FBI number: 90 percent
- Percentage error: +7 percent

Whites killed by whites

- Graphic: 16 percent
- FBI number: 82 percent
- Percentage error: −66 percent

Whites killed by Blacks

- Graphic: 81 percent
- FBI number: 15 percent
- Percentage error: +66 percent[30]

As for the police statistics in the graphic, there isn't an official database that compiles the percentage of each race the police have killed. So, those particular statistics in the graphic are dubious, at best, or completely fabricated, at worst.

Despite this graphic being roundly debunked in 2015, I wrongly assumed it was dead. But after George Floyd's murder, five long years later in 2020, this odious pseudo-infographic returned to life like a post-apocalyptic zombie and was enjoying another viral run. When I mentioned that I'm very familiar with the disinformation graphic, it's because I had this graphic thrown in my face on a near-daily

30 Jon Greenberg, "Trump's Pants on Fire tweet that blacks killed 81% of white homicide victims," https://www.politifact.com/factchecks/2015/nov/23/donald-trump/trump-tweet-blacks-white-homicide-victims/.

basis on social media during the summer of 2020. Bad faith actors demanded that I "quit crying" about George Floyd and focus on the out-of-control epidemic of Black-on-Black crime that this graphic laid out in clear detail. It was emotionally exhausting to fight against this piece of disinformation multiple times a day, and even writing about this image now brings back a feeling of low-grade PTSD.

In our journey to unite behind a civil world, we must be aware that the fraternal twins, misinformation and disinformation, will be powerful nemeses hell-bent on keeping us divided. It already isn't a fair fight, and to add to the unfairness, figuratively speaking, the twins now have nuclear weaponry at their disposal with the rapid advances in artificial intelligence as a powerful deception tool. More than ever, we will need to understand the enemy and prepare for their attacks and ensure that we don't fall into the trap of using them ourselves.

Let's start with identifying the problem.

Outsmarting Misinformation and Disinformation

Thankfully, as powerful as misinformation and disinformation can be, they can both be beaten with proper due diligence and thoughtfulness. Here are a few simple ways to stay a step ahead of fake news.

Verify, Verify, Verify!

Before sharing anything on your social media channels, pause for a moment, and ask yourself some simple verification questions. What is the originating source of the content? Is it a reputable source of news? If it's coming from an individual's account, is that person an expert, or at least, credible? If you are unsure, go through their previous posts and articles and see the type of content that they're posting. If any of it is making you raise an eyebrow and think "I'm not sure this person/source is legit," then don't amplify the damage done by the mis/disinformation by sharing it any further. This cannot be said enough: *Just because a piece of content aligns with your political and social views doesn't mean that it's true.*

Also, use independent, nonpartisan fact-checking websites like Politifact.com, FactCheck.org, or Snopes.com to verify whether the claims being made are true. Equally as important, if it's clear that someone in your network is spreading misinformation or disinformation, use the verified information from the fact-checking websites to debunk their claims in real time. There's no guarantee that doing so will change any hearts and minds, but even if it gets someone to think twice before sharing the content with their network, then you have officially made the world a better place through your actions.

Last thing on this—if you have made the mistake of sharing something, only to later verify that what you shared is untrue, please don't just delete the post and pretend that nothing happened. Own your mistake, publicly state why the post you shared was untrue, and hopefully your actions will serve as an example of how to deal with this effectively.

Read Laterally, Not Vertically

Stanford University researchers Sam Wineburg and Sarah McGrew, coauthors of the working paper "Lateral Reading: Reading Less and Learning More When Evaluating Digital Information," sampled forty-five individuals on their ability to determine the credibility of digital information. Specifically, they observed ten PhD historians, ten professional fact-checkers, and twenty-five Stanford University undergraduates, and the findings were fascinating.[31]

In one example, the participants were asked to evaluate the credibility of two organizations: the American Academy of Pediatrics and the American College of Pediatricians. Despite the similar sounding names, that's where the similarities end.

The American Academy of Pediatrics has been in existence for nearly a century, and they are the largest professional organization of pediatricians in the world. Similar to most credible professional organizations, they offer continuing education and publish a journal. The American College of Pediatricians, on the contrary, is a splinter group that broke from its parent organization over the issue of adoption by same-sex couples. According to the research study, their extreme anti-LGBTQ stances—which include a post that suggested the addition of the letter *p* for pedophile to the acronym LGBT, since pedophilia is "intrinsically woven into their agenda"—helped to earn them the designation of a hate group that is "deceptively named" and acts to "vilify gay people" by the Southern Poverty Law Center.[32,33]

Getting back to the observation, the study participants were asked to read an article about bullying on both websites and then evaluate the trustworthiness of each website as a source for information about the topic. It's worth noting that according to the Centers for Disease Control and Prevention (CDC), nearly 40 percent of high

---

31 Sam Wineburg and Sarah McGrew, "Lateral reading: reading less and learning more when evaluating digital information," https://papers.ssrn.com/sol3/papers.cfm?abstract_id=3048994.

32 American College of Pediatricians, 2002, https://www.splcenter.org/fighting-hate/extremist-files/group/american-college-pediatricians.

33 Ryan Lenz, "American College of Pediatricians defames gays and lesbians in the name of protecting children," March 1, 2012, https://www.splcenter.org/fighting-hate/intelligence-report/2012/american-college-pediatricians-defames-gays-and-lesbians-name-protecting-children.

school students who identify as lesbian, gay, or bisexual, and about 33 percent of those who were not sure of their sexual identity, experienced bullying at school or electronically in the last year, compared with 22 percent of heterosexual high school students.[34] Sadly, the American College of Pediatricians implied that programs to reduce bullying against LGBTQ students amount to "special treatment" and that these programs may "validat[e] individuals displaying temporary behaviors or orientations." Conversely, the American Academy of Pediatrics article focused more inclusively on factors that might place youth at risk for bullying, such as sexual orientation, weight, race, and income.

It should be clear which organization should be considered more credible when it comes to advocating against the destructive nature of bullying, right? Well, maybe not. After the study participants spent ten minutes (five minutes per website) to evaluate the trustworthiness of each source, here's what Wineburg and McGrew found. The PhD historians believed that both websites were trustworthy sources for information about bullying, whereas the undergraduate students overwhelmingly found the American College of Pediatricians website to be a more trustworthy source for information about bullying. But here's where it gets interesting: the professional fact-checkers *unanimously* found the American Academy of Pediatrics website to be a more trustworthy source about bullying.

So, what did the professional fact-checkers see that the others didn't in such a short period of time? Largely, the historians and the students read *vertically*, meaning that they stayed within the article to evaluate its credibility. The professional fact-checkers read *laterally*, meaning that they left the original article and examined additional

34 Centers for Disease Control and Prevention, "Fast facts: preventing bullying," https://www.cdc.gov/violenceprevention/youthviolence/bullyingresearch/fastfact.html.

pages like the "About Us" and the "Resources" pages and conducted additional web searches to determine the reliability of both websites. In doing so, they were able to quickly discover a significant amount of information that revealed the American College of Pediatricians to be a far less credible source to speak on the topic of bullying than the American Academy of Pediatrics.

Like a professional fact-checker, we must apply the same effort when evaluating the credibility of information online. Before taking an article on a website at face value by solely reading vertically, do the requisite due diligence of reading laterally. In addition to scrutinizing the "About Us" and "Resources" pages on the websites that you visit, investigate their social media presence, and conduct Google searches to learn more about the organization or the author. Is it more effort to do this? Definitely, and that's precisely why so few people do it. As mentioned earlier, if we're going to unite people around the goal of creating a kinder and more civil world, we must consistently take uncommon action and encourage as many people as possible to do the same.

Cross-Reference Other Sources

If you're reading a piece of news on social media that seems unlikely to be true, an excellent best practice is to cross-reference the story against other reputable news sources. A tragic example of this was when news broke all over social media in January 2020 that Los Angeles Lakers legend, and my all-time favorite basketball player, Kobe Bryant—and eight other people, including his daughter Gianna—died in a helicopter crash.

The news seemed so outlandish and off the wall that I ignored it initially as social media clickbait foolishness and went on with my day. After a few hours of seeing that this story wasn't going anywhere, and now my friends and family were texting me about it, I decided to check some reputable news sources that confirmed my fears that the story was indeed true.

Cross-referencing is an effective strategy because if it's a big enough story, you can believe that every reputable news outlet on earth will be publishing it on their websites or airing it on their networks. However, if you're reading a piece of social media content that *seems* like incredibly important news (e.g., a huge political scandal or a celebrity death) and when you cross-reference it against other outlets, no one else seems to be covering it, that's likely a sign that the source material isn't true.

Also, if a story has links to support their claims, investigate them to see if they lead to reputable and credible news sources (pro-tip: if you're on a computer, instead of clicking the link and possibly being led to an unsafe website, hover over the link with your mouse to see the source). One thing that misinformation and disinformation both do exceptionally well is use the right combination of words to activate us emotionally and get us to spread fake news without thinking first. If you're feeling outrage overload or anxiety overload by a social media post or a news headline, consider that as your body's alarm system to get you to pause and search to see if this story is true by cross-referencing it online. If you don't find anything that supports the story's validity, exhale and move on.

Understanding—and ideally, defeating—misinformation and disinformation is a critical aspect of our civility work, but we're still just getting started. Now it's time to move past thinking and into the nuanced challenges of communication.

Roll up your sleeves, my friend—there's a lot of work still to be done.

INTENTIONAL CONSISTENT INTERVENTION #14: *STAY HUMBLE*

Remaining open-minded about our beliefs and our worldview is a key characteristic of a person who is willing to engage fully in creating a more civil world. Are you intellectually humble?

ICI Steps:

1. Choose a polarizing topic on which you have a strong opinion (e.g., abortion, gun control, or immigration). Write it down in your *Civil Unity Journal*.
2. Refer to Duke University's *General Intellectual Humility Scale* and rate yourself on how closely each of the following statements describes you on a five-point scale ranging from "not at all like me" to "very much like me":
   - I question my own opinions, positions, and viewpoints because they could be wrong.
   - I reconsider my opinions when presented with new evidence.
   - I recognize the value in opinions that are different from my own.
   - I accept that my beliefs and attitudes may be wrong.
   - In the face of conflicting evidence, I am open to changing my opinions.

- I like finding out new information that differs from what I already think is true.

In your *Civil Unity Journal*, answer the questions, "Based on my responses to the General Intellectual Humility Scale statements, do I believe that I am intellectually humble? Why or why not?"

3. Whether you answered "No" or "Yes" to the question on step two, commit to asking yourself on a daily basis, "Is it possible that I could be wrong about my opinion on this polarizing topic?" Follow up by staying curious and learning more about the topic from credible sources.

INTENTIONAL CONSISTENT INTERVENTION #15: *VERIFY, VERIFY, VERIFY!*

Verify content before sharing it on social media and potentially contributing to the spread of mis/disinformation.

ICI Steps:

1. Before sharing anything on social media, pause and answer the following questions in your *Civil Unity Journal*:
    - What is the originating source of the content?
    - Is it a reputable source of news? Why or why not?
    - If the content is from an individual's social media account, is that person an expert or at least credible? Why or why not?

2. If any of your answers to the questions in step 1 cause you to question the credibility of the content, do not share it and potentially spread mis/disinformation. Remember, just because a piece of content aligns with your political and social views doesn't mean that it's true.
3. If you accidentally end up sharing a piece of mis/disinformation (we've all been there), please own it by stating publicly that what you shared was incorrect and why it is untrue.

INTENTIONAL CONSISTENT INTERVENTION #16: *READ LATERALLY*

Instead of reading articles vertically, commit to channeling your inner professional fact-checker by reading laterally.

ICI Steps:

1. Find an online article that is interesting to you, and read it in its entirety.
2. After reading the article, visit the "About Us" and "Resources" pages on the article's website. In addition, Google the author and investigate the author's social media presence.
3. Ask yourself, "Do you believe the author is credible? Why or why not?" Record your answers in your *Civil Unity Journal*.
4. Repeat this process once a week to keep your lateral reading skills sharp.

INTENTIONAL CONSISTENT INTERVENTION #17: *CROSS-REFERENCE*

Similar to ICI #15, before sharing content on social media, it is critical to pause and cross-reference the story against other news outlets to see if it's true first.

ICI Steps:

1. Before sharing any salacious news-related content on social media from individual accounts or from a group's social media page, pause to notice how the story is making you feel. If the content is causing you to experience outrage overload or anxiety overload, chances are that the story could be sensationalized to inspire that reaction from you, or worse, the story could be completely untrue. In your *Civil Unity Journal*, write down an example of a social media post or story that you wanted to share with your network. In addition, in your journal answer these questions:
    - Why did you want to share the story?
    - What value did you think it would bring to your network?
    - Ultimately, did you share the story with your network? Why or why not?
2. Cross-reference the story against legitimate, established, and reputable news sources to see if they have reported on the story. If they haven't, that could be a good sign that the original story is not true. It's always better to take your time to gather the facts before

sharing (which means, you'll never be the first person to share the news with your network), as opposed to needing to be the first person to share the breaking news and potentially spreading mis/disinformation. In your *Civil Unity Journal*, document the legitimate, established, and reputable news sources that you will use to cross-reference the validity of social media posts and stories. Also, answer in your journal why you believe your selected sources are credible.

3. If you do not find any supporting stories on other news outlets, point out to your social media connections who are sharing the story on their social media accounts that it has not been officially verified. That may not get them to stop sharing the potentially false story, but even if one person decides not to share it, your actions have officially made the world a better place.

CHAPTER 6
Changing How We Think

Teachers open the door, but you must enter by yourself.

—CHINESE PROVERB

While the year 2020 is thankfully a distant memory for most of us because of the misery of the COVID-19 pandemic, for me, it will be remembered for a different kind of virus—one of the social media variety.

On May 25, 2020, Minneapolis police officers arrested a Black man named George Floyd for allegedly attempting to buy cigarettes with a counterfeit $20 bill. What ensued was police officer Derek Chauvin cruelly and dispassionately kneeling on Mr. Floyd's neck for over nine agonizing minutes. This episode was replayed over and over in the news, and it was wreaking havoc on my mental health.

It didn't help that three months earlier, a Black man named Ahmaud Arbery was shot and killed by three men in a racially motivated hate crime while jogging through a suburban neighborhood outside of Brunswick, Georgia. Then, less than three weeks later, Breonna Taylor, a Black emergency medical technician (EMT) was shot and killed by police officers during a botched raid on her home in Louisville, Kentucky. And to top it off, just a few hours before George Floyd's murder, a Black man named Christian Cooper was bird-watching in the Ramble of Central Park in New York City when a white woman named Amy Cooper (no relation) called in a false accusation to the police claiming that Mr. Cooper threatened her life. In reality, all he asked her to do was leash her dog so that he could bird-watch in peace. Add in that all of this was happening during the beginning of a global pandemic, and my mental health was in tatters.

By the time I watched George Floyd's agonizing murder where he began to cry out for his dead mother as he slowly suffocated, that was the proverbial final nail in my mental wellness coffin. Strangely, during this time, I had many of my white friends ask me why I was so upset about this. It's not like I knew Mr. Floyd, so why was I so despondent? Since I'm a writer, I took to my personal Facebook account less than a week after Mr. Floyd's murder to share my personal thoughts about being Black in America with anyone who cared to read them. Next is what I wrote in its entirety along with the accompanying image of me, my youngest daughter, Nia, and our dog, Ace.

Little did I know that posting this on social media would change my life forever.

Why I Never Walk Alone

Twice a day, I walk my dog Ace around my neighborhood with one, or both, of my girls. I know that doesn't seem noteworthy, but here's something that I must admit:

I would be scared to death to take these walks without my girls and/or my dog. In fact, in the four years living in my house, I have never taken a walk around my neighborhood alone (and probably never will).

Sure, some of you may read that and think that I'm being melodramatic or that I'm "playing the race card" (I still have no clue what that even means), but this is my reality.

When I'm walking down the street holding my young daughter's hand and walking my sweet fluffy dog, I'm just a loving dad and pet owner taking a break from the joylessness of crisis homeschooling.

But without them by my side, almost instantly, I morph into a threat in the eyes of some white folks. Instead of being a loving dad to two little girls, unfortunately, all that some people can see is a 6'2" athletically-built Black man in a cloth mask who is walking around in a place where he doesn't belong (even though, I'm still the same guy who just wants to take a walk through his neighborhood). It's equal parts exhausting and depressing to feel like I can't walk around outside alone, for fear of possibly being targeted.

If you're surprised by this, don't be. We live in a world where there are a sizable amount of people who actually believe that racism isn't a thing, and that White Privilege is a made-up fantasy to be politically-correct. Yes, even despite George Floyd, Christian Cooper, Ahmaud Arbery, and Breonna Taylor (and countless other examples before them, and many to come afterward), some people still don't seem to get it.

So, let me share some common sense points:

1. *Having white privilege doesn't mean that your life isn't difficult, it simply means that your skin color isn't one of the things contributing to your life's difficulties. Case in point, if it never crossed your mind that you could have the cops called on you (or worse, possibly killed) for simply bird-watching then know that is a privilege that many Black and brown people (myself included) don't currently enjoy.*
2. *Responding to "Black Lives Matter" by saying "All Lives Matter" is insensitive, tone-deaf and dumb. All lives can't matter until Black lives matter.*
3. *Racism is very real, and sadly, some people have deluded themselves into thinking it's limited to the*

fringes of the hard-core MAGA crowd. As Amy Cooper proved, it's just as prevalent in liberal America as it is anywhere else.

4. *While racism is real, reverse-racism is not. Please don't use that term, ever.*
5. *In order for racism to get better, white allies are absolutely critical. If you're white and you've read this far, hopefully you care enough to be one of those allies. Please continue to speak up (despite some of your friends and family rolling their eyes at you), because your voices matter to PoC [People of Color] now more than ever. Special shoutouts to many of my friends for doing it so well.*
6. *And if you're white, and you're still choosing to stay silent about this, then I honestly don't know what to say. If these atrocities won't get you to speak up, then seriously, what will? Also, it's worth asking, why stay connected to me on social media? If you aren't willing to take a stand against actions that could get me hurt or killed, it's hard to believe that you ever cared about me (or, my mission to make the workplaces kinder and more compassionate) in the first place.*

As for me, I'll continue to walk these streets holding my 8-year-old daughter's hand, in hopes that she'll continue to keep her daddy safe from harm.

I know that sounds backward, but that's the world that we're living in these days.

The Aftermath and the Need to Change How We Think

For reasons that I will never quite understand that post ended up going viral. At last count, that post was shared over 580,000 times, had nearly 80,000 comments, and was read by millions of people all over the world. I was asked to appear on major network television morning shows and other large media outlets to discuss the post.

Many people post on social media in hopes of going viral, but in my case, I didn't ask for, or want, any of this. All that I wanted to do was share my raw and unfiltered thoughts in hopes that it would be cathartic in processing my vicarious trauma. Instead, it served as an unforgettable reminder that anything that gets shared online could be seen by the entire world.

While most people who saw my post sent me kind, loving, and thoughtful messages, there was a small percentage of folks who sent me diabolically vile messages and phone calls. If you break down the numbers, when millions of people see a social media post, even if only 1 percent of those folks feel inclined to engage in hateful behavior, that still amounts to tens of thousands of people. The messages ranged from being called "nigger" more times in a month than I have in my entire life up to that point to receiving death threats. To this day, I'm still not clear how reading that post evoked such a response.

Years later, looking back on it, the mean-spirited messages from my viral post not only reignited my desire to create a more civil world (so, to the haters, thanks, I guess?), but it also drove me to passionately examine the nuances of human behavior. Admittedly, I didn't dive too deeply into the sociopathic insanity of the messages that I received in hopes of holding together my fragile mental health at the time, but I did notice a theme in many of them.

First, they were rife with logical fallacies: "If all of your neighbors are evil racists, then why don't you move to an all-Black neighborhood, or better yet, back to Africa?" When did I say that all of my neighbors were evil racists? And no, I'm not going to move, thanks. Second, they were riddled with implicit biases: "Well, most people who commit crimes in suburban neighborhoods kind of look like you do. You can't blame people for not feeling safe and wanting to protect their property and loved ones." So, do I need to wear my office clothes when I'm taking a walk around my neighborhood in order to make you feel safe?

Yes, all of this is awful, obviously, and I hope you're not surprised by any of this. But let's dig a little deeper. If you think about most of the incivility and disrespectful disagreements in the world, I'm willing to bet that logical fallacies or implicit biases play a sizable role in making our disagreements worse.

To create a more civil world, it's clear that we must change how we habitually think. Specifically, we need to master two things: (1) knowing what to do when people use logical fallacies and succumb to implicit biases during our conversations with them, and (2) equally as important, we need to make sure that we have our houses in order regarding both issues so that we're not unwittingly adding to our problems.

There's a lot of ground to cover, so let's get to it.

Recognizing Logical Fallacies

Logical fallacies are arguments that may sound strong or convincing on the surface but, upon deeper scrutiny and the application of critical thinking, can be proven invalid because of their faulty logic. This can become especially problematic when logical fallacies are used as tools to manipulate conversations, which erodes any chance of civil discourse, finding common ground, or trying to create sincere understanding.

There are literally hundreds of logical fallacies, but here are a few of the most common examples:

Ad Hominem Fallacy

Ad hominem is a Latin phrase that means "against the man." This fallacy is when a person avoids addressing the argument and instead attacks the person who is making the argument.

Person A: "We really need to improve the culture of our workplace. I'd like to share some suggestions on how we can do this."

Person B: "Wait a minute … haven't you been divorced twice? Why would we listen to your suggestions when you've repeatedly proven that you can't even improve the culture in your own home?"

Anecdotal Fallacy

This fallacy uses an individual's limited personal experience as evidence that a larger primary argument is valid.

Person A: "I'm so excited to visit my friend in Los Angeles next weekend!"

Person B: "Whatever you do, don't drive in that city."

Person A: "Why do you say that?"

Person B: "I visited Los Angeles five years ago for business, and after being on the road for only twenty minutes, someone rear-ended me while she was texting on her phone. The drivers in that city are awful."

Appeal to Authority Fallacy

This fallacy uses the authority (real or imagined) of personas as the primary reason to support an argument, without providing any additional reasoning. This is especially problematic if the authority isn't an expert in the area being discussed.

Person A: "Why are you investing all of your retirement funds into that cryptocurrency company?"

Person B: "Because my favorite NFL player endorsed them, and he's a smart guy who is known for making great decisions on the football field. I'm confident that he knows what he's doing with this company too."

Appeal to Ignorance Fallacy

This fallacy claims that something is true because there's no evidence against it.

Person A: "You keep saying that the bartender is in love with you. Why do you think that?"

Person B: "Because she hasn't told me that she isn't in love with me."

Bandwagon Fallacy

This fallacy argues that the popularity of an idea is the primary determinant of the idea's validity. To be clear, if many credible experts believe in an idea's validity, that would not be considered a logical fallacy.

Person A: "Why are you putting your pre-workout powder in your mouth and trying to swallow it without using any water? That looks weird and unsafe."

Person B: "It's called 'dry scooping' and all of the fitness influencers are doing it."

Burden of Proof Fallacy

This fallacy is similar to the Appeal to Ignorance fallacy, but it's more annoying because the person making the claim is placing the burden on *the other person* to disprove their claim instead of providing evidence on their own.

Person A: "You're saying that we all have a magical axolotl who follows us in the spirit realm and influences our daily choices? Can you prove that?"

Person B: "Can you prove that it's *not* true?"

Person A: "Wait, what? Umm … no, I can't, but …"

Person B: "Exactly. You have no proof that it's not true. Thanks for proving my point."

False Dilemma Fallacy

This fallacy reduces complex and nuanced arguments into a "black and white" issue with only two options while ignoring that other options exist. It's a form of mental laziness.

Person A: "I'm against this war."

Person B: "If you're against the war, that means that you're against our troops and you're against America."

False Equivalence Fallacy

This fallacy states that two things are equivalent because they share some characteristics while ignoring the significant differences between the two.

Person A: "You need to wear a shirt and shoes before entering the restaurant."

Person B: "How dare you try to take away my freedoms! This is what it must have been like to endure a life of chattel slavery in the pre-Civil War south."

Red Herring Fallacy

This fallacy diverts attention from the real problem by using an irrelevant point to avoid focusing on the original issue.

Person A: "Dr. Jones has been posting some very hateful content on her social media channels lately, and a lot of us are deeply concerned about it. Hiring her as the chair of the department would be a problematic move. Take a look at this Islamophobic rant that she posted yesterday." *<Shows Person B the phone.>*

Person B: "Dr. Jones is one of the most accomplished physicians on the East Coast, and her research is unparalleled. Her work has positively affected the lives of countless people all over the world, and as a potential chair of the department, she will be able to do so much good for the department, our hospital, and our community."

Slippery Slope Fallacy

This fallacy argues that one action will set off a series of events that will lead to extreme and undesirable circumstances.

Person A: "I think Uncle James just gave Tyler a sip of his wine."

Person B: "WHAT?! Tyler is only nine years old! What if he develops an insatiable taste for it and decides to raid our liquor cabinet while we're asleep one of these nights? He could become an alcoholic by the time he turns eleven, a middle school dropout by thirteen, and sleeping under a bridge at fifteen! Uncle James is trying to ruin Tyler's life and any possibility for future success and happiness!"

Straw Man Fallacy

This is one where a person misrepresents, distorts, or exaggerates your argument to make it easier to attack. It's called a "straw man," because instead of addressing your actual argument, they are creating a flimsier version that's easier to beat up.

Person A: "I don't feel comfortable with my ten-year-old daughter taking an Uber by herself all the way across Los Angeles at night."

Person B: "So, you think that girls are too frail and helpless to take care of themselves without a man like you there to protect them? Is that what you want your daughter to grow up believing?"

Tu Quoque Fallacy

Tu Quoque is Latin for "you also," and it's a form of an *ad hominem* argument. This fallacy is used to avoid engaging with the primary argument by pointing out the potential hypocrisy of the person making the argument. It's a form of whataboutism.

Person A: "Snorting cocaine is terrible for your health, and I don't want you going anywhere near that stuff."

Person B: "Dad, you sniffed lines when you were my age and you're in great health now. Cocaine can't be *that* terrible."

There are so many of these that I could write a separate book on this topic, but I'll stop here for now. These logical fallacies are used frequently in bad faith arguments, and if you watch political debates on TV, you could play a drinking game by taking a shot of your favorite liquor whenever a candidate uses one to prove their point. Actually, scratch that—I don't want this book to be a cause for your inevitable hospitalization if you do so.

So, how do we deal with this? We'll have to HIT them with logic.

Addressing Logical Fallacies with HIT

As mentioned, there are countless logical fallacies out there for us to deal with, and we're going to need some sound strategies to deal with the avalanche that threatens to bury us daily. Allow me to introduce a simple acronym named HIT that could prove helpful for you.

- How do you know that?
- Identify logical fallacies.
- Test their argument.

How Do You Know That?

My late father was a brilliant man. Not only did he earn his PhD at a very young age and was a college professor for many years, but he was also extremely emotionally intelligent. There are so many traits that I admired in my dad, but the one that I've come to love the most was a trait that I used to find to be the most annoying.

My dad was a philosopher at heart, and, oftentimes, when I stated something that I firmly believed in, he would respond with a loving but challenging question:

Me: "I hate multivariable calculus. There is no chance that I'll ever use this stuff in the real world."

Dad: "Really, Shola? How do you know that?"

Me: "Because there's no reason for me to ever use it, that's why!"

Dad: "But you're only nineteen years old and a sophomore in college. How would you know that you will never use it for the rest of your life?"

Me: *<mumbling obscenities under my breath as I slink away>*

"How do you know that?" was a potent question that rocked my confidence and reminded me to remain intellectually humble. I didn't understand it at the time, but my dad wasn't simply interested in my opinion on matters; he was very interested in how I processed information and how I arrived at thoughtful, logical conclusions. My dad realized that the last thing that our world needs are more people spouting off opinions without thinking about them first. Instead, he wanted to raise critical thinkers, and after his death, I still look back at this simple question as one of the greatest gifts that he ever left me.

Let's put this question into action. Imagine that you have a neighbor named Brad who believes that the Earth is flat. This is more than a passing thought for Brad. My guy is committed to this idea, and he's ready to argue the merits of it with you. This is the time to use this simple question to make him pause and evaluate the strength of his argument.

Brad: "It's obvious that the Earth is flat. Only brainless sheep believe that the Earth is round."

You: "You said that the Earth is flat. How do you know that?"

Brad: "There is a lot of proof. I'm part of an online forum with scientists who have stated confidently that the Earth is flat, and that the 'Round Earth' idea is a hoax."

YOU: "Interesting. I want to better understand how you came to the conclusions that the Earth is flat and that the Earth being round is a hoax. Since you said that there is a lot of proof, surely you can share some of it with me."

We will continue this conversation momentarily, but this question is the entryway to determine if Brad's argument is on sound footing or not, so we must begin here. More importantly, this question is used to help Brad to become self-aware about how he came to that conclusion.

For now though, let's put Brad aside and talk about us. Surely, we have formed conclusions on a number of issues too, right? Take a look at this list of hot-button topics:

- Abortion and/or when life begins
- Transgender athletes in sports (or LGBTQ+ rights in general)
- The stability of our democracy
- Censorship or "cancel culture"
- Diversity, Equity, and Inclusion (DEI) being taught in our schools and workplaces
- Banning books in libraries
- Immigration and the security of the southern border
- The threat of climate change
- The conflict in the Middle East
- Gun control and the Second Amendment
- The safety or dangers of artificial intelligence
- Healthcare as a right or a privilege

- The merits, or lack thereof, for animal testing
- The safety and/or efficacy of vaccines
- Labor unions as a positive or destructive force in the workplace
- Religion being allowed in our schools
- The need, or lack of need, for police reform
- The effectiveness of affirmative action
- The merits or dangers of marijuana legalization
- The viability of Social Security
- The utility and/or morality of the death penalty
- Your political party
- People in the other political party

Think of your most deeply held conclusions from this list. If I were to ask you, "How do you know that?" would you be able to answer this question to credibly defend your conclusion? Responding with "the 8 p.m. anchor on my favorite cable news station said so" isn't going to cut it. Part of creating a more civil world is the willingness to enter potential disagreements in good faith. The ability to deeply reflect on the question, "How do you know that?" is an excellent starting point.

Identify Logical Fallacies

Let's return to Brad and his conclusion that the Earth is flat. We started by asking him how he came to this conclusion. If his argument is sound, it should be free from logical fallacies. However, if you happen to spot one (or numerous ones), you'll need to point them out to him.

You: "Interesting. I want to better understand how you came to the conclusions that the Earth is flat and that the Earth being round is a hoax. Since you said that there is a lot of proof, surely you can share some of it with me."

Brad <Burden of Proof Fallacy>: "Like I said, there's a ton of it. I'm not going to do the legwork for you. Google is your friend; use it."

You: "Hold up, Brad. You made the claim that the Earth is flat, and when I asked you to provide some proof, you turned it on me by asking me to find it for you. Why should I have to search for the information to back up your claim?"

OR

You: "Interesting. I want to better understand how you came to the conclusions that the Earth is flat and that the Earth being round is a hoax. Since you said that there is a lot of proof, surely you can share some of it with me."

Brad <Appeal to Authority Fallacy>: "Dr. Johannson has a PhD in philosophy and is a leading expert in this field. I've been following him online for years, and his insights on Flat Earth Theory are impeccable. I'm happy to share his research with you."

You: "Awesome, thanks—I'm interested in seeing his research. However, stating that the Earth is flat is a big claim, and leaning on the research of one person doesn't mean that it's necessarily true. Also, I'd love to learn more about why you consider Dr. Johannson to be an expert in this field."

This step in the HIT process requires an understanding of logical fallacies and how they can render arguments invalid. The idea is that by respectfully introducing how the presentation of Brad's argument is flawed can help him to question the validity of his argument. Part of our critical thinking process is to also ensure that we're not using logical fallacies as the rickety foundation for our conclusions as well. Again, think of your most deeply held beliefs and ask yourself if they would hold up against thorough examination and scrutiny.

Test Their Argument

This is the final step in the HIT process, and the idea is to get the person to test the validity of their conclusion—ideally, by asking a question.

You <Burden of Proof Fallacy>: "Hold up, Brad. You made the claim that the Earth is flat, and when I asked you to provide some proof, you turned it on me by asking me to find it for you. Why should I have to search for the information to back up your claim?"

Brad: "Because the proof is everywhere, and it's annoying that I need to prove something that's readily available and plainly obvious."

You: "If I made the argument that unicorns exist, and you asked me to back up my claim, would you accept it if I said that it was obvious, but provided no proof, and told you to find the evidence of unicorns on your own?"

Brad: "That's different and you know it. We're not talking about unicorns; we're talking about real life."

You: "We're both sharing conclusions—in my case unicorns, and in your case, flat Earth—but neither of us is offering proof. Without providing credible evidence, I'm having a hard time considering your argument, just like you're rightfully not considering my unicorn argument. Are you willing to share any evidence with me? If not, I'm always down to discuss this again if you're willing to do so."

OR

You <Appeal to Authority Fallacy>: "Awesome, thanks—I'm interested in seeing his research. However, stating that the Earth is flat is a big claim, and leaning on the research of one person doesn't mean that it's necessarily true. Also, I'd love to learn more about why you consider Dr. Johannson to be an expert in this field."

Brad: "As mentioned, he is highly educated, very smart, and he has been discussing that the Earth is flat on his social media account for years. He has a huge following and a lot of people believe in him. You should check him out."

You: "Will do. But it sounds like Dr. Johannson is not an expert in a field that is relevant to the Earth being round or flat. Not to mention, having a large social media following doesn't necessarily guarantee expertise either. I'm just trying to understand how you came to this conclusion. Can you elaborate?"

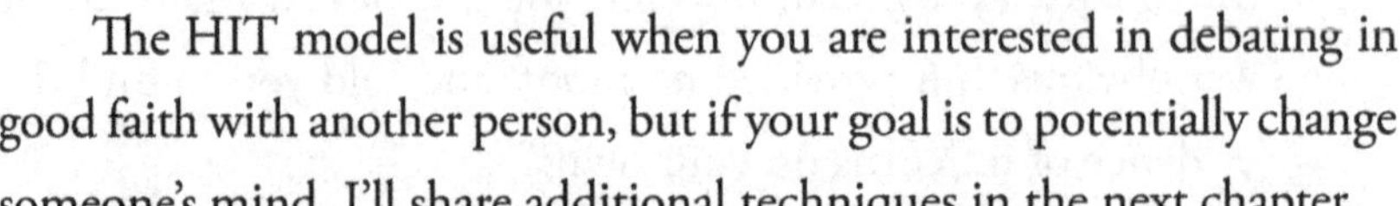

The HIT model is useful when you are interested in debating in good faith with another person, but if your goal is to potentially change someone's mind, I'll share additional techniques in the next chapter.

We've covered the first hurdle; now we have to leap over the second one.

Overcoming Implicit Bias

The final challenge in changing our thinking is to overcome implicit bias.

Logical fallacies and implicit bias are similar in the sense that they both can contribute to breakdowns in communication and the creation of a less civil world, but how they do so is distinctly different. Logical fallacies are when arguments are flawed because of a problem with its structure, reasoning, or content. Implicit bias is when the attitudes or stereotypes that we hold about other people or a group of people affect our judgments, decisions, and actions, often outside of our conscious awareness (that is why it's also known as unconscious bias). In other words, logical fallacies are a philosophical challenge, whereas implicit bias is a psychological one. And because we need to fix what's in between our two ears, it's safe to say that I saved the hardest one for last.

Unlike being susceptible to misinformation and disinformation or trafficking in logical fallacies, every living person has implicit bias. In a sense, our biases serve a necessary survival function. In order to process the dizzying amount of information that's bombarding our brains in any given moment, we must effectively categorize information quickly and efficiently to prevent overloading our conscious thought and becoming overwhelmed. This has its advantages as well as disadvantages.

Beneath the surface, we all hold some form of bias around the following characteristics:

- Age
- Ethnicity
- Gender identity

- Physical ability
- Physical appearance (height, weight, or attractiveness)
- Political affiliation
- Race
- Religion
- Sexual orientation
- Socioeconomic status

We may believe that we don't hold biases about people in the groups above, but science has not only shown that we do, but we also often behave in opposition to our conscious beliefs about people. Worse than that, our conscious values are not as effective of a predictor of our future behavior as our implicit biases.

We may believe in gender equity, but assume that the woman who walks into the boardroom is the administrative assistant and not the CEO of the company. We may believe that during the hiring process that we are looking for the best person to do the job but unconsciously dismiss the gray-haired man whose age doesn't fit what we have predetermined for the ideal candidate. We could attend equality marches and donate money to causes that fight against racism but see a Black man holding his cell phone at nighttime in our neighborhood and reflexively call the police because we assume that he's holding a gun.

Overcoming the influence of implicit bias is very hard work that is going to require unceasing vigilance and awareness, so let's start by outlining the common forms of implicit bias.

Affinity Bias

This refers to the tendency to unconsciously favor people who are similar to us in some way. This often leads us to have greater empathy, respect, and trust for people who share the same characteristics that we have.

Example: In the grocery store, you may see a man raising his voice and being rude to the cashier, but since he reminds you of your Uncle George, you're willing to give him the benefit of the doubt. However, if the exact same behavior was exhibited by someone outside of your affinity group, you would be appalled.

Attribution Bias

This refers to the tendency to unconsciously judge others based on their actions while unconsciously judging ourselves based on our intent.

Example: If one of our colleagues is consistently running late for meetings, we may judge her as irresponsible, disorganized, or disrespectful. However, if we have been late for three meetings in a row, we would explain it as being overscheduled and not that we are irresponsible, disorganized, or disrespectful.

Confirmation Bias

This refers to the tendency to unconsciously seek out and favor information that aligns with our preexisting beliefs while giving less credence to the information that doesn't. It's the idea that human beings don't seek out information as much as they seek out validation.

Example: If we have determined that cats make better pets than dogs, our brains will unconsciously seek out news, social media posts, and information that support our beliefs. In addition, we will give less credence to the enormous evidence that dogs are also amazing companions.

Conformity Bias

Also known as "group think," this refers to when your views are unconsciously swayed by the opinions of the other people in the group rather than forming their own judgments.

Example: If we see others in our class cheating on an exam, we may unconsciously feel like it's OK to do the same thing, even if our personal values have determined that cheating is wrong.

Halo Effect

This refers to the tendency to unconsciously view a person in a positive light after discovering one impressive trait about them.

Example: You just found out that your new neighbor graduated from an Ivy League school, so you assume that she must be intelligent, ambitious, and a hard worker (which may or may not be the case).

Horns Effect

This is the opposite of the Halo Effect. It is the tendency to unconsciously view a person in a negative light after discovering one unpleasant trait about them.

Example: You're a lover of animals, and you found out that your dinner date spends his free time on the weekends attending dog fights. Because of this, you assume that he's soulless, cruel, and irredeemably sociopathic (which may or may not be the case).

Similar to the logical fallacies, there are many more implicit biases than these, and I encourage you to discover more. For now, let's figure out how we're going to overcome these biases.

Addressing Implicit Bias with FLOW

As mentioned, overcoming our implicit biases is going to take a lot of work. Having a process that we can lean on will be enormously helpful, and FLOW is a model that can help with that. Unlike the HIT model, which is a step-by-step process, FLOW consists of four distinct strategies that you can use in any order or combination to help reduce your susceptibility to implicit bias:

- **F**amiliarize
- **L**earn
- **O**bserve
- **W**hy

Familiarize

One of the reasons why the Affinity Bias has such a strong hold on our minds is because many of us don't hang out socially with people who are different from us. According to a poll by Reuters/Ipsos, American social groups aren't very diverse. According to the research, about 40 percent of white Americans have only white friends, and 25 percent of non-white Americans only have friends of their own race.[35] Without the benefit of personal exposure to different races, sexual orientations, ethnicities, or religions, we are primarily left with stereotypical narratives from the media to shape our opinions of these groups for us. I hope you're with me on how problematic that could be if we're hoping to create a more civil and unified world.

Intentionally familiarizing ourselves with folks from different backgrounds is a critical action to mitigate the effect of implicit bias on our brains. One thing that I know for sure is that our biases grow and thrive in the distance between us and the groups we are biased against. With distance, we can believe that certain groups of people are threats to our way of life, less worthy of kindness, and sadly, feel a twisted sense of pleasure when they are harmed. We are social beings who depend on the connection of our fellow humans, and that's why it's very difficult to maintain our biases when we increase the proximity. As my mama loves to say, "It's hard to hate people from close up."

The effort to surround ourselves with diverse individuals, whether it's through travel, networking at work, social events, church, sports and recreation, or volunteering, truly has the power to unite the world. Not only does it provide us with the opportunity to shift inaccurate and potentially harmful beliefs about others, but it also helps to rewire our brains and provide us with positive examples of people who are different from us.

Embrace the challenge of familiarizing yourself with people outside of your affinity group and become comfortable with the initial discomfort of doing so.

---

35 Lindsay Dunsmuir, "Many Americans have no friends of another race: poll," August 8, 2013, https://www.reuters.com/article/2013/08/08/us-usa-poll-race-idUSBRE97704320130808/.

Learn

A few years ago, my neighbor and dear friend (who, for context, is white) asked me for a favor that seemed completely innocent. He was on vacation with his wife, and he texted me and said, "Hey, Shola, we're on vacation, and we're not going to be home until next week. We have a bunch of Amazon packages stacked up outside of our front door. Do you mind grabbing them from our front porch and bringing them back to your house? We'll pick them up from you once we get back. Let me know!"

What was my response to my buddy's request? "Aww, HELL NO!"

As a Black man in America, there is *no chance* that I'm going to go to a house that's not mine, pick up a stack of packages that do not belong to me, and then carry them up the street to my house. That could end up very poorly for me, and that is not a risk I'm willing to take. After sharing my concerns with him, he responded by saying, "Damn, that's a great point." We had a laugh about it over drinks once he returned home from vacation, and he learned something that he was previously unaware of.

Not only does this small example demonstrate the beauty of familiarizing ourselves by having a diverse friend group, but also the second strategy in the FLOW model, which is to constantly learn. And by learn, I'm talking about learning about others and ourselves.

Because implicit bias affects everyone, regardless of our race, gender identity, age, political affiliation, or country of origin, we must commit to the challenge of ongoing learning, or else the specter of entropy will shove us into the grave of biased thinking and behavior without us even knowing.

I have two practical suggestions on how to do this. If you are committed to familiarizing yourself with others by diversifying your friend group, take the next step by learning from them. Specifically, learn about their challenges, their fears, their concerns, and their ideas about what a better future could look like. In addition, I recommend learning about the history of equality movements in America and throughout the world. Not only does it build empathy and understanding of others, but it is also one of the most effective bridges to a more civil and unified world. Education is a life-altering and civility-enhancing force, and I caution you to be very wary of anyone who wants to limit or restrict educating others about history. Education is more than the intellectual exercise of learning from our past; it also actively plays a critical role in ensuring that the most harmful aspects of our history are not repeated.

Second, we must learn about the biases that we currently hold. Again, as mentioned, no one is free from a bias-free mind. Knowing this, it is essential that we learn what our biases are so that we can increase our awareness of our behavior when we are in a situation that could activate those biases.

One of the best tools to assist us in this pursuit is the Implicit Association Test (IAT) created by Project Implicit, a nonprofit organization of researchers in the field of implicit social cognition. As of this writing, you can head over to their website and take an IAT for free on several potential implicit bias areas, such as race, religion, sexuality, gender identity, physical ability, and weight, to name a few.[36] The test is simple in its premise. According to Project Implicit, the goal of the IAT is to measure the strength of associations between groups (e.g., Black people or gay people) and evaluations (good or bad) or stereotypes (athletic or clumsy). In addition, the IAT attempts to assess biases that are not necessarily personally endorsed and may

36 https://implicit.harvard.edu/implicit/takeatest.html.

be contradictory to what one consciously believes. In my personal opinion, the IAT is one of the best tools available to do so.

Like any tool, the IAT is not foolproof, but it can serve as an excellent addition in our repertoire in learning more about ourselves and our potential blind spots so that we can work diligently toward a more compassionate and self-aware world.

Observe

Over ten years ago, I remember sitting in a doctor's office waiting room, and I witnessed a tender scene of loving compassion. There were two women—an older woman and a younger woman—standing together in a warm embrace. The younger woman just finished her appointment and was very distraught. She lowered her head as she slowly walked toward the older woman, and the younger woman began sobbing uncontrollably into the older woman's arms. Together in the middle of the waiting room, they held each other as the older woman stroked the younger woman's hair and lovingly consoled her.

As I watched the situation, I thought to myself, "Thank goodness that this young woman has her mom here to support her through this difficult time." Almost immediately afterward, the older woman kissed the younger woman on the forehead and walked toward the front desk as the younger woman sat down next to me. I awkwardly offered my condolences for what she was going through as she wiped her tears with her sleeve. She replied graciously, "Thank you. I don't know if I'd be able to get through this situation if I didn't have my wife with me. She's my emotional rock."

Her wife? For reasons that I didn't understand at the time, my implicit bias erroneously assumed that these two women were mother and daughter. After looking at them both again with clear eyes, they both looked far closer in age than I initially assumed, with the only difference was that the "older" woman's hair had streaks of gray in it. I still shudder thinking about how I could have made an already bad situation cataclysmically worse if I called her loving wife "her mom" as she continued to sob in the waiting room.

That may not seem like a life-changing story, but it was for me. As a presumably open-minded and thoughtful guy, it rocked me that I made such a dumb leap of abstraction based on insubstantial evidence. On a positive note, that moment started me on my journey to learn more about implicit bias and specifically the third technique to help mitigate the effects of it.

Our brains are constantly trying to make meaning of the world around us by creating associations and generalizations, and our biases can serve as effective shortcuts in doing both. Sometimes that can be useful, but oftentimes, it's not. That's why after that waiting room moment, I've reminded myself to primarily focus on *what I'm able to observe*, without adding additional narratives to the story of which I have no clue about. Were they mother and daughter? Married to each other? Best friends? Newly chosen tributes for the reaping in the next *Hunger Games*? I had no idea about any of that until the woman kindly told me the truth. Prior to her doing so, the only facts that I observed were two women sharing a compassionate moment together, and that's it.

Dispassionately observing the world means that we are engaging in the challenging practice of choosing facts over our feelings. This is critical when dealing with overcoming the unconscious pull of our biases. The waiting room scenario is a relatively benign example, but our inability to prioritize the facts over our feelings by focusing solely on what we're observing could have deadly consequences.

For example, there are many people who unconsciously choose their feelings over the facts when deciding to call the police over a perceived threat. But what if they could slow down for a moment and focus solely on what they are observing instead of their feelings? A few years ago, a participant in one of my Implicit Bias training sessions at the University of California at Irvine emailed me a brilliant flowchart of how this could be done. A version of it is below.

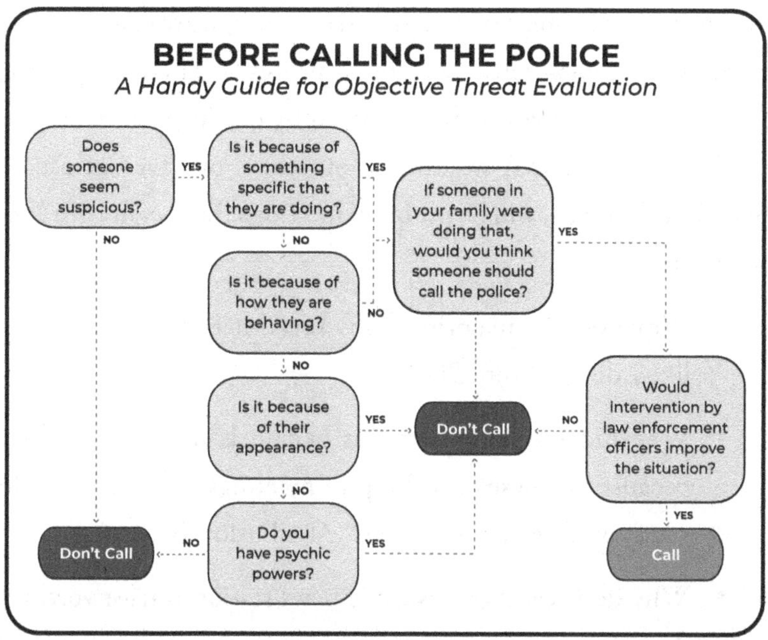

This flowchart powerfully demonstrates how slowing down and focusing on what we are able to observe (instead of our feelings) could prevent an unnecessarily disastrous outcome because of biased thinking. The Observe strategy is simple but not easy. Whenever you find yourself attempting to make sense of a situation by adding unnecessary narratives, pause and ask yourself, "Are these facts or are these my feelings?" If it's the former, then act accordingly. If it's the latter, pause and then take the necessary steps to objectively evaluate what you are observing.

Why

The last strategy in the FLOW model requires a significant amount of self-awareness. Despite our best efforts to remain fair, objective, and unbiased, it's likely that our implicit biases will find a way to rise to the surface every now and then. That's why we need to ask ourselves why we are making the decisions we're making and, of course, only answer with the facts. Having a trusted friend or colleague who can challenge our decision-making can accelerate the process of discovering whether or not we're unconsciously being driven by our implicit biases.

The questions that we can ask ourselves, or have our accountability buddy ask us, will be probing questions that begin with "why." For example:

- Why does the majority of my social network look/pray/vote like I do? (Affinity Bias)
- Why did I assume that this person is not very intelligent because he doesn't speak up in meetings, when I often don't speak up in meetings either? (Attribution Bias)
- Why do I feel that this cable news station is trustworthy but the other ones are not? (Confirmation Bias)
- Why are we administering less pain medication to Patient B than Patient A, even though they both presented with the same symptoms? (Conformity Bias)
- Why do I feel that my fellow college alumnus would be a better fit for our work team than the other candidates? (Halo Effect and/or Affinity Bias)
- Why do I not trust a person with a low credit score to babysit my child? (Horns Effect)

In some cases, the right questions may uncover if implicit bias is driving our decision-making or not.

Addressing logical fallacies and overcoming implicit bias are two vital methods to change how we think and to encourage civil discourse. Even though "The Work" section of this book is coming to an end, please don't think that there isn't more work to be done. The hardest work that we will likely encounter on our civility journey involves the healing of ourselves and others—and that's coming up next.

Are you ready?

INTENTIONAL CONSISTENT INTERVENTION #18: *HIT THEM WITH LOGIC*

There are many logical fallacies that derail civil discourse, and you will need to be able to spot them, so you can address them using the HIT model.

ICI Steps:

1. Familiarize yourself with the bulleted list of common logical fallacies listed next and the definitions and examples on pages 154–159:

    - Ad Hominem Fallacy
    - Anecdotal Fallacy
    - Appeal to Authority Fallacy
    - Appeal to Ignorance Fallacy
    - Bandwagon Fallacy
    - Burden of Proof Fallacy
    - False Dilemma Fallacy
    - False Equivalency Fallacy
    - Red Herring Fallacy
    - Slippery Slope Fallacy
    - Straw Man Fallacy
    - Tu Quoque Fallacy

    The goal of doing this is twofold: (a) to ensure that you can spot any one of these fallacies when they are used in an argument and (b) to ensure that you are not using any of these arguments yourself.

2. When presented with a logical fallacy, use the HIT model to hopefully increase the other person's self-awareness about their shaky argument:
    - Ask, "How Do You Know That?"
    - Identify the Logical Fallacy
    - Test Their Argument
3. In your *Civil Unity Journal*, reflect back on what it was like to use the HIT model in a conversation. Was it easier than you thought it would be, harder than what you thought it would be, or pretty much what you expected? How did the other person respond? Document your answers in your journal.

INTENTIONAL CONSISTENT INTERVENTION #19: *GO WITH THE FLOW*

Just like the previous ICI, there are many implicit biases that will derail not only civil discourse but the quality of our thinking as well. To avoid that outcome, we must become aware of our implicit biases and use the FLOW model to mitigate the effect of them.

ICI Steps:

1. Familiarize yourself with the bulleted list of common implicit biases given next and the definitions and examples on pages 169–171:
    - Affinity Bias
    - Attribution Bias
    - Confirmation Bias

- Conformity Bias
- Halo Effect
- Horns Effect

2. To remain vigilant against implicit biases, it is critical to apply the strategies in the FLOW model as often as possible:

   - ***Familiarize***: Take inventory of your inner social circle—does everyone in your inner circle look like you, love like you do, pray like you do, and vote like you do? If so, sometime in the next thirty days, step out of your circle, and commit to personally interact with people of different races, sexual orientations, gender identities, ethnicities, religions, or political parties. Record your personal observations in your *Civil Unity Journal*.
   - ***Learn***: Visit the Implicit Association Test website and take a free test (https://implicit.harvard.edu/implicit/takeatest.html). In your *Civil Unity Journal*, write down your immediate thoughts about the test. Were you surprised by your results? Why or why not?
   - ***Observe***: In your *Civil Unity Journal*, write down one strategy that you will use to get you to slow down, interrupt any biased thinking, and refocus on the objective facts of the situation as opposed to your subjective feelings about the situation.
   - ***Why***: In your *Civil Unity Journal*, identify a person who will serve as your accountability buddy and will

ask you challenging "Why" questions to uncover any potential biased thinking.

3. After having the opportunity to apply all four of the FLOW strategies, ask yourself, "Which of the four strategies of the FLOW model has been the most helpful in helping me to address my implicit biases, and why?" Document your answer in your *Civil Unity Journal*.

PART 3

THE HEALING

CHAPTER 7

We Don't Need to Change the World to Change the World

One cannot deny the humanity of another without diminishing one's own.

—JAMES BALDWIN

There were two iconic television programs that were on in my house on every weekday growing up in Amherst, Massachusetts. The first one was *The Price Is Right*, where the legendary host Bob Barker introduced me to the importance of paying attention to good deals when shopping at the grocery store and to spay and neuter my pets. I'm calling my shot; if I ever end up on *The Price Is Right*, I will win the Showcase Showdown.

The second iconic television program was *The Oprah Winfrey Show*. Unlike *The Price Is Right*, which came on in the late morning, I was able to watch *The Oprah Winfrey Show* in its entirety on most days because it came on after school. Oprah's fearless interviewing style, thought-provoking topics, insightful commentary, and warm demeanor made her a role model for me, and she still is to this day. In 1988, though, there was a particular episode that was different from any episode of her show to that point or ever since. It is not hyperbole to say that this one-hour episode not only was burned into my consciousness, but it also ended up changing both Oprah's iconic show and me forever.

On this episode of the show, Oprah invited a panel of white supremacists who identified themselves as "Skinheads"—a neo-Nazi hate group known for spreading white supremacist propaganda—to her show, in hopes of exposing their ignorance to the world.[37] Unfortunately, for Oprah and for her viewers, the show took a hard left turn when the episode devolved into an hour-long infomercial for their despicable and evil ideology and beliefs.

One memorable moment from the episode was when Oprah confronted one of the white supremacists about the fact that he refuses to sit next to Black people because he viewed them as monkeys. When Oprah pressed him on his "monkey" statement, he condescendingly responded by saying, "It's a proven fact." Similar hateful, ignorant,

37 https://www.youtube.com/watch?v=5BRDSvO_eDA.

and mean-spirited comments were spewed throughout the episode, before the white supremacists decided to storm off of the stage during a commercial break. Once the show returned from break, and the stage was empty, an understandably shaken Oprah said to the studio audience, "I agree with this woman down here who said, 'I have never seen such or felt such evilness and such hatred in all of my life.'"

Neither had I.

I was thirteen years old at the time that I saw this episode, and it shook me to my core. At this stage in my development, I was fully aware of the depressing reality that some people wouldn't like me because of the color of my skin, but this was the first time when I realized that there were people out there who wanted to *hurt or kill me* because of the color of my skin. Naïvely as a thirteen-year-old, I believed that racial violence wasn't a thing anymore, and that it was a relic of the transatlantic slave trade, or more recently, the Jim Crow South. There are days when I wish that I could go back in time and hug the younger version of myself who was so innocent and sincerely shocked that I could be harmed just for existing. That episode broke my heart, and from that point on, I became hypersensitive of my race, fearful of any white men with shaved heads (because they reminded me of the white supremacists on Oprah's show), and perpetually anxious about being a victim of violence because of it.

Oprah, who, more than anyone, fully realizes the immense power and influence of her platform, made a commitment after that episode to drastically change the course of her show, forever. Eighteen years later, in 2006, Oprah reflected on that fateful episode of her iconic show by saying, "I realized in that moment that I was doing more to empower them than I was to expose them. And since that moment, I've never done a show like that again." Her show continued to be a force for positively transforming lives, and the best was yet to come.

In *The Oprah Winfrey Show*'s final season in 2011, twenty-three long years after the airing of the infamous Skinhead episode, Oprah invited two of the white supremacists from that show, Dave Mazzella and Mike Barrett, back to discuss how their lives have changed since this episode. The 180-degree transformation was astonishing.

The conversation began with Dave offering an effusive, and long-overdue, apology to Oprah for how they behaved on her show twenty-three years ago. In a measured, calm, and thoughtful manner (none of which could be used to describe his younger self who appeared on her show over two decades ago), Dave owned his behavior by saying, "We were rude, we were arrogant, we were disruptive, and hateful … and I just apologize, first and foremost, to you … for the evil we expressed."

The apology was immediately and graciously accepted by Oprah, who then went on to ask Mike what he thought when he saw the footage of his younger self from the show. The question clearly made Mike emotional, and as his eyes started to get glossy, he quietly said through a shaky voice, "It really brings tears to my eyes. That kid was lost."

A year after his initial appearance on *The Oprah Winfrey Show*, Mike was sent to prison for defacing a synagogue, and he had an epiphany while he was there. "The crew they put me on was entirely Black. Including a Black sergeant. So, here I am, the only white guy … these guys accepted me for who I was. They already knew about my past because it was tattooed all over my back and my neck. I had swastikas all over me and things like that. But they treated me like a human being. And it just taught me that everybody's a human being, and we just can't hate people."

Then it was Dave's turn to share his epiphany. Six months after the original show aired, he recruited a group of white supremacists in Portland, Oregon, who ended up murdering an Ethiopian student, and it took that terrible act to wake him up from his hate-induced slumber. After having his epiphany, Oprah followed up by asking, "Do you feel better as a human being now?" Dave responded by sheepishly saying, "Oh, most definitely. I feel differently, I'm so embarrassed ... obviously, watching things like that. Embarrassing being here today because of my past, I don't like it, and it's humiliating."

When I finally got around to watching the reunion episode, I was nearly forty years old, and more importantly, I was now a parent of two little girls. The combination of receiving some proof that the world has become a little kinder and safer for my daughters and seeing how much those two men had transformed made me very emotional. They were contrite, self-aware, respectful, and, in my opinion, sincerely sorry. My faith in humanity was reinforced, and I began to embrace a life-affirming idea that I previously dismissed for most of my life: even the most lost souls among us are capable of change.

Changing a Few Hearts and Minds

You might have read the story of the two white supremacists and not have been moved in the slightest. Maybe you're thinking, "Wait, Shola, you're celebrating two convicted felons—one who defaced a synagogue and another who participated in the murder of an innocent Ethiopian student—because they finally saw the light two decades later?! Miss me with this silly 'hero's journey for racists' bullshit, please."

No, this isn't about celebrating them. This is about *studying* them. These two men were radicalized with beliefs that were deeply entrenched in their identity, and somehow, they were able to free themselves from that toxic cesspool of hate and leave their old identities behind. This is worthy of unpacking. One thing we should be able to agree on is that the world is unquestionably a better place with Mike and Dave awakened from their hateful stupor than it would be if they were still terrorizing marginalized communities and recruiting others to do the same. We are going to spend a significant amount of time in this chapter discussing how this change occurred, and Mike gave a hint earlier in his answer to Oprah.

Before we get there though, a critical aspect of creating a more civil world is the belief that people have the capacity to change. It may be easier to view groups of people whom we don't like or agree with as monolithic, or worse, irredeemable, but is that generally true? Yes, there are unquestionably people who are so hateful that they can't be reached, but I believe that percentage is far smaller than most people believe. You wouldn't be blamed if you watched Dave and Mike's depravity on Oprah's show in 1988 and believed that they were beyond saving, because that was certainly my belief. But if so, we both would have been dead wrong, and that's what is so fascinating about this. If these two extremely unlikely people could change their hearts and minds without being violently beaten into submission, isn't it possible that others could potentially enjoy a similar outcome?

Optimistically, if you are interested in changing the world, there are two pieces of good news: (1) it can be done nonviolently, and (2) we won't have to change as many hearts and minds as we may think to make it happen. Harvard Kennedy School academic dean, professor, and author Erica Chenoweth's (they/them pronouns) TEDx talk, "The Success of Nonviolent Civil Resistance," describes their shocking data on the efficacy of nonviolent resistance.

> I collected data on all major nonviolent and violent campaigns for the overthrow of a government or a territorial liberation since 1900. The data covered the entire world

> and consisted of every known case where there were at least one thousand observed participants; this is hundreds of cases. Then I analyzed the data, and the results blew me away. From 1900 to 2006, nonviolent campaigns worldwide were twice as likely to succeed outright (than) violent insurgencies. And there's more. This trend has been increasing over time, so that in the last fifty years, nonviolent campaigns are becoming increasingly successful and common, whereas violent insurgencies are becoming increasingly rare and unsuccessful.

I know we're not talking about overthrowing governments in this book, violently or otherwise, but the research does throw ice-cold water on the commonly held belief that violence is the most effective means of making lasting, widespread change. Violence as a means for positive change has a terrible track record of success, whether it's beating a misbehaving child with a belt, verbally assaulting someone with whom you vehemently disagree, or deciding to storm the nation's Capitol in hopes of reversing the results of an election. If we are serious about meaningful change, the most effective means of doing so is to leave the violence behind.

Chenowith wasn't finished dropping eye-opening gems in their TEDx talk:

> Researchers used to say that no government could survive if just five percent of its population rose up against it. Our data showed that the number may be lower than that. No single campaign has failed during that time period after they had achieved the active and sustained participation of just 3.5 percent of the population. And lots of them succeeded with far fewer than that. 3.5 percent is nothing

> to sneeze at—in the U.S. today, that's like eleven million people. But get this: every single campaign that surpassed that 3.5 percent was a nonviolent one.[38]

I know that I'm taking some significant liberties here, but what if we applied this to making lasting changes to our civil discourse? Could getting 3.5 percent of the population to *actively and collectively* participate in nonviolent communication over a sustained period of time positively change our global discourse? That's a bet that I'm willing to make.

The art of opening up hearts and minds to different viewpoints is unquestionably hard work. If you're up for the challenge, let's address a common pitfall before we get to the solution.

Avoiding the Boomerang

Take a look at the following interaction. Be real with me—how likely is it that a contentious conversation about gun control will end like this?

Person A: "No one is going to tread on me by taking away my second amendment rights! If you want to take away my guns, I dare you to swing by my house and try."

Person B: "News flash, you mouth-breathing, ammo-sexual, hillbilly. No one is coming for your stupid guns. The government has more things on their plate than trying to take away your sole source of overcompensation for your inability to please your wife."

Person A <thoughtful pause>: "Yes, you are right. This is insightful feedback, and I'm grateful that you have inspired me to look

38 https://www.youtube.com/watch?v=YJSehRlU34w.

> within. Not only am I paranoid and delusional, but thanks to your accurate and astute commentary, it's clear that I'm also using my guns to self-soothe for my numerous bedroom failures. I appreciate your candor, and I vow to do better."

As we both know, there's a better chance of a fiery asteroid from the Andromeda galaxy crashing through the roof of your home in the next five minutes than there is of Person A ever responding in that way to Person B's less-than-kind comment. There is a fascinating reason for this.

In most cases, attacking a person only serves as fuel to double down on the person's commitment to their cause and harden their belief. This social psychology phenomenon is often known as the Boomerang Effect or reactance theory. This theory was first proposed by Jack Brehm in 1966, where if behavioral freedoms are reduced or threatened with reduction, the individual will be motivationally aroused to regain them.[39] In other words, it's when a strong attempt to change someone's attitude "boomerangs" and results in the opposite of the intended effect. This makes sense because most people want to maintain their sense of autonomy, and when someone is trying to forcefully change how they think or act (or worse, attack them for it), it feels like an assault on their freedom, so they rebel against it.

When I was in college, I remember a nearby house off campus with a big yard sign that said in all capital letters with multiple exclamation points, "DON'T BE AN ASS!!! STOP PLAYING LOUD MUSIC!!!" Can you predict what happened regularly when people drove by that house? Yep, the windows were rolled down, the bass was thumping as they drove by, and like clockwork, people did the

---

39 Jack W. Brehm, "A theory of psychological reactance," 1966, https://psycnet.apa.org/record/1967-08061-000.

opposite what the house owners hoped for. I'm convinced if the sign said, "Please be considerate and lower the volume," that would have been a far more effective strategy.

One would assume that the Boomerang Effect is common sense, but based on the current discourse online and offline, it seems like owning the other side, claiming intellectual or moral superiority over them, and hurling personal insults at them are the go-to tactics to try to change minds. The problem with these strategies, as we both know, is that they don't work, and they never have.

Perhaps you're thinking, "So wait … are you suggesting that I shouldn't forcefully call out problematic behavior that's harming others? If a person is a trash juice human who is doing trash juice things, then they need to know about it. Sorry, not sorry."

I'm all for addressing problematic behavior, but *it's how it's done* that is critically important if you care about your efforts being useful. If your goal is to use personal insults to dunk on the misguided people who don't see the world in the way that you do, at least mindfully do so knowing that you're really only accomplishing three things:

1. You are deepening the person's commitment to the beliefs and/or behaviors that you find repugnant.
2. You have set fire to any chance of the person seeing the merits of your position.
3. You are actively contributing to the unproductive discourse that's destroying our world right now.

If you're fine with those three points, then please continue to do you. On the contrary, if we are serious about changing problematic behaviors, we're going to need to do more than satiate our poor impulse control and our lizard-brain need to be right. Thankfully, there's a better way.

The Key to Bridging Ideological Divides and Disagreeing More Effectively

When Mike was recounting his time in prison to Oprah, he said that one thing that led to his epiphany was that the Black prisoners "treated me like a human being." That might not seem like a noteworthy statement, but I can safely say that one thing that unites people is the need to have their humanity seen and acknowledged. In Mike's case, it was enough to spark his metamorphosis from a hateful neo-Nazi to a contrite and repentant member of society. The key is finding some common ground, even when we believe none can be found. As painfully simple as this may sound, this is the most effective means to bridge ideological divides and disagree more effectively.

Let's return to the gun control conversation and explore how attempting to find common ground can potentially change the energy of the conversation.

Person B: "Another mass shooting! I'm sick of this crap. We're the only country on the planet that is dealing with this insanity. Anyone who owns a gun is a paranoid and delusional whack job who needs psychiatric help. If I could buy a giant electromagnet to hover over the earth, and all of the guns in the world would float into outer space never to be seen again, that would be a dream come true."

Person A: "I feel you. I'm horrified by this latest mass shooting, just like you are."

Person B: "Yeah, sure you are. I know that you own guns, so you probably aren't *that* horrified."

Person A: "No, please trust that I'm absolutely horrified by this, and we agree that there's nothing positive about innocent people being killed. And yes, I do own guns. We probably also agree that protecting our freedoms is important too, right?"

Person B: "Of course. In particular, I'm concerned about the freedom to walk into a shopping mall without fearing that I'll be shot, or my kids having the freedom to go to school without having to do active shooter drills. Why is your freedom to own a weapon of war more important than our freedom to exist in peace?"

Person A: "We agree that it's not more important. I also want to see these mass shootings end, and I also want to live in a world where active shooter drills in schools are a relic of the past. As a responsible gun owner, I believe these things can happen while still maintaining my freedom to own a firearm, but it will take a lot of work for us to get there. Most importantly, I understand how distressing this is, because I'm feeling the same way. We can and we must do better."

Person B: "Yeah, we have to do something, because I'm sick of this. I hate guns and I don't see any purpose for a civilian to own a semiautomatic weapon. I'm with you that there is a lot of work that needs to be done, because these weapons should not be available to people who are willing to kill innocent people."

A few things about this conversation. First, Person A didn't launch into any personal attacks toward Person B about being a "radical socialist/fascist/Marxist" (or whatever the insult of the day is) in response to the bizarre suggestion that all guns should disappear into outer space. Instead, Person A focused on the common ground that they both shared—specifically, being horrified about the shooting, protecting our freedoms, and that something needs to be done about this. Second, when Person A "lowered the temperature" by remaining calm, it increased the likelihood of Person B doing the same so that they could engage in a productive conversation about an emotionally charged topic, which wouldn't have happened if Person A responded angrily with personal attacks. Third, even though no minds were changed in this conversation, Person A did provide contrary evidence to Person B's biased belief that all gun owners are "paranoid and delusional whack jobs" and that maybe Person B has more in common with Person A than originally assumed.

Please don't get me wrong here—this isn't about being polite for politeness' sake, because that accomplishes nothing. The civility that I'm advocating for has little to do with good manners and common courtesy. It's about the hard and uncommon work required to *create the space for potential change to happen*. Thoughtful, passionate, and respectful debate is how we can bring change to the world. And, as mentioned earlier, it may take less people than we thought to do this.

Also, the art of finding common ground isn't limited to gun control. Remember this list of hot-button topics from chapter 6?

- Abortion and/or when life begins
- Transgender athletes in sports (or LGBTQ+ rights in general)
- The stability of our democracy
- Censorship or "cancel culture"
- Diversity, Equity and Inclusion (DEI) being taught in our schools and workplaces

- Banning books in libraries
- Immigration and the security of the southern border
- The threat of climate change
- The conflict in the Middle East
- Gun control and the Second Amendment
- The safety or dangers of artificial intelligence
- Healthcare as a right or a privilege
- The merits, or lack thereof, for animal testing
- The safety and/or efficacy of vaccines
- Labor unions as a positive or destructive force in the workplace
- Religion being allowed in our schools
- The need, or lack of need, for police reform
- The effectiveness of affirmative action
- The merits or dangers of marijuana legalization
- The viability of Social Security
- The utility and/or morality of the death penalty
- Your political party
- People in the other political party

Despite how divisive these issues can be, finding common ground is very possible, if you are willing to search for it. Regardless of which side of the argument that you find yourself on, here are a few things that most reasonable people can agree as common ground:

- We all deserve to live in peace.

- We all should have the freedom to pursue our best lives.
- We all should enjoy safety for ourselves and our family.
- We all should experience equality.
- We all should have our humanity seen and acknowledged.

The key word in the previous paragraph was *reasonable*. Unfortunately, there are unreasonable people who have no interest in finding common ground, and we need to be able to spot those bad actors quickly so that we don't waste any of our precious time or energy with them.

The Bees, the Flies, and the Ants

In my nearly fifty years traveling around the sun, I have experienced and personally heard a lot of wild things:

- "Transgender people aren't human."
- "I'm not getting on a flight with a towel head; they're all terrorists."
- "I don't want that gay guy teaching my kid. He's going to groom my son to be like him."
- "The Jews are vermin who need to be exterminated from the earth."
- "Immigrants only bring crime and disease to our country and offer no positive benefit whatsoever."
- "People who vote with (choose a political party) are all evil and deserve to burn in hell."

<Sigh>.

There's an old saying that goes, *honeybees don't waste a moment of their time trying to convince houseflies that honey tastes better than shit.* There are some deeply closed-minded people out there walking among us. Does it make sense to try to find common ground with the people who are drawn to the shittiness of intolerance, as opposed to the sweetness of civility? Well, that depends.

For argument's sake, I'll group people into three categories:

Honeybees: Civility Champions

These are the people who are committed to bringing more civility to this world and will keep actively working at it until it happens. Hopefully, dear reader, you are in that camp. Thankfully, there is no need to spend our time working on finding common ground with these folks, because they already embrace the importance of bringing more civility to our discourse and inspiring others to do the same.

Houseflies: Unreasonably Closed-Minded

These people are the ones who are tethered tightly to their hateful and ignorant beliefs and likely will not be moved by any efforts to find common ground. So, is it worth it to even try to find common ground with them? As mentioned earlier, it depends.

Is the person a loved one? Is it someone who you have to interact with frequently, whether you want to or not? If so, then it's worth a try. Mike and Dave are proof that a 180-degree turn in one's perspective is possible, even when it is unlikely. However, if your attempt to find common ground fails, then it makes sense to set a boundary and move on. For example:

Person A: "The transgender agenda is disgusting. These people just need to go away and stop parading their sick lifestyle in my face. They can all burn to death in a fire as far as I care."

Person B (Attempt to find common ground): "Uncle Fred, I find that very offensive. I'm sure we agree that the trans community are human beings who deserve to live in peace and be treated with respect, right?"

Person A: "Sorry that you're offended by the truth. There is no universe where these subhuman perverts deserve to live in peace or be treated with respect."

Person B (set boundary): "You're entitled to your opinion, but since you're currently in my house, I don't want you to speak like that here in front of my kids. If you do, I'll ask you to leave. In our house, we respect the humanity of others."

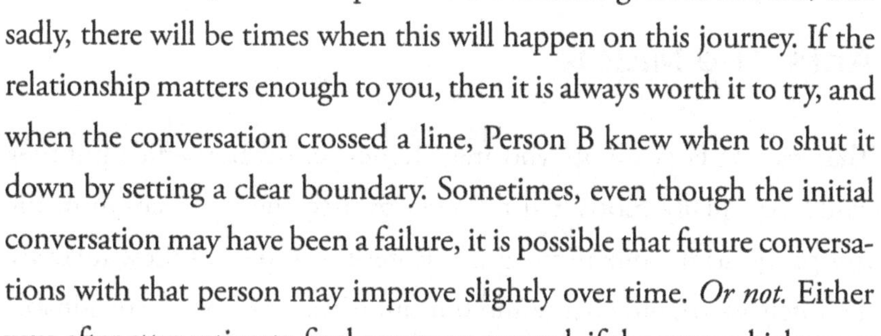

In this case, the attempt to find common ground fell flat, and sadly, there will be times when this will happen on this journey. If the relationship matters enough to you, then it is always worth it to try, and when the conversation crossed a line, Person B knew when to shut it down by setting a clear boundary. Sometimes, even though the initial conversation may have been a failure, it is possible that future conversations with that person may improve slightly over time. *Or not.* Either way, after attempting to find common ground, if the person kicks your effort aside and responds with bad faith arguments and a fully closed mind, it's probably best to save your breath and move on.

On a related note, there are times where it doesn't make sense to even attempt to find common ground. I remember a time when I was at a party in college, and similar to one of the white supremacists on Oprah's show, there was a guy who was making comments within earshot that Black people were basically monkeys. Should I have pulled him aside and calmly said, "Hey man, I'm sure that we agree on the fact that we're both human beings, right?" Yeah, no thanks. Why would I try to engage in a respectful conversation with someone who doesn't even see my humanity? In addition, since I'm a lover and not a fighter, I wouldn't consider responding to his hateful comment with violence, but what if I did? As mentioned earlier with the Boomerang Effect, if I did succumb to my lesser angels by punching him in the face, not only would I have solidified his belief (and anyone else at the party who shared in his belief) in my lack of humanity, but I probably would have been expelled from school.

Since this housefly wasn't someone whom I cared about or someone I would likely ever see again, I decided to ignore his ignorance and let it go. Some people are not worth costing us our energy, our words, and our mental health. The sooner we can distinguish who those people are, the better.

Ants: The Middle

That leaves a large group who aren't honeybees or houseflies, but they could be equally motivated to crawl over to the honeycomb in the tree or the stinky pile in the grass. Enter the ants, and these folks are definitely worth our energy and our time. These people are reasonable and willing to engage in good faith discussions, even if you both don't see eye-to-eye on certain issues. Everything in this book up to this point is about influencing these folks by leading by example.

Specifically, this means modeling civil communication by staying calm, critically thinking, checking our biases, disagreeing without disrespect, and finding common ground. Engaging in these actions consistently is the fastest and the most effective means of reaching the hearts and minds of others.

And we are going to need to positively influence as many hearts and minds in the middle as we can. If there's a chance that it only takes moving the needle 3.5 percentage points to positively transform our discourse, our lives, and our world, it behooves us to commit fully to this effort.

INTENTIONAL CONSISTENT INTERVENTION #20: *THE COMMON CURE*

Resist the impulse to attack and demean others (which solves nothing), and instead seek to cure our ailing discourse by finding common ground.

ICI Steps:

1. When engaged in a tense disagreement, instead of attacking or insulting the other person, try to find common ground. If necessary, also use ICI #1 (Setting the Ground Rules) in your efforts to keep the conversation respectful. Document in your *Civil Unity Journal* the common ground that you found with the other person.
2. If no common ground can be found (which will happen), accept it, cut your losses, and move on.
3. Ask yourself, "Did finding common ground with the other person improve the energy of the disagreement? Why or why not?" Document your answers in your *Civil Unity Journal.*

CHAPTER 8

Workplace Toxicity, Intolerance, and Radicalization

Always go with the choice that scares you the most, because that's the one that is going to require the most from you.

—CAROLINE MYSS

One very hot afternoon after facilitating a half-day workshop for the leaders of a large midwestern university, I headed out of the venue where my ride to the nearby airport was waiting for me. The driver greeted me politely, took my suitcase, and opened the door for me to sit in the back seat—all of which I greatly appreciated.

I can't speak for other keynote speakers and workshop facilitators, but when I'm done with an event, I'm exhausted. Because I'm an energetic guy on stage, once the event is over, it takes everything within my power just to keep my eyes open afterward. The driver was clearly in the mood to chat, and since he started by talking about my favorite topic, the NBA, it was enough to keep me engaged and awake during the short trip to catch my flight.

The conversation was lively, and during the ride, the driver asked me if I needed water, and I responded, "Yes, please." The driver then asked me if the music on the radio was too loud, and I responded, "No, it's fine." When he sensed that I might be hot in my business suit, he turned up the air conditioning in the car, and I excitedly responded, "Thank you sir, that's exactly what I needed!"

After my enthusiastic response to my driver turning on the AC, our lively conversation awkwardly paused, and I could sense that the driver wanted to say something to me. Moments later, my instincts were proven correct.

"Hey man, do you mind if I ask you something? I hope that you don't get offended."

Sidenote: can we agree that nothing good ever comes after someone saying, "I hope that you don't get offended"?

Reluctantly, I replied with a sigh of resignation knowing that my peaceful car ride would likely come to an end once these words left my lips, "Sure, what's up?"

"Why can't more Black folks be polite like you?"

Ugh. I did not ask for this.

Part of the reason why I wrote this book is because I suffer from a lifelong condition known as "Hindsight Brilliance." That's a fancy way of saying that I always have the best and most thoughtful responses to these situations, but they always come to me an hour or two after the interaction is over, which, obviously, does me no good.

Despite the combination of exhaustion, Hindsight Brilliance, and knowing that I had only less than ten minutes left before arriving at the airport, I was able to direct a six-word question at the driver that raised his awareness of the inappropriate nature of his question while not having to expend any of my energy in the process.

We'll return to this interaction later in this chapter, where I'll share that magical question. But first, we need to be equipped with the strategies to navigate some of the most difficult interpersonal challenges in existence.

Extremely Difficult Situations

Ever since that fateful car ride, I asked my workshop attendees, email list subscribers, social media followers, and friends, what are the discussions where it is the hardest to remain civil? There were a lot of answers, but generally, they could be grouped into these themes:

1. Incivility of the Workplace
2. Incivility of Intolerance
3. Incivility of Radicalization

In addition to applying everything that we have learned up to this point, we'll also need to employ some new techniques to navigate these choppy waters, starting with #1.

1. The Incivility of the Workplace

There are many people who are struggling to find civility in the workplace, and the statistics support that. According to the American Psychological Association's (APA) 2023 Work in America Survey, 19 percent of respondents stated that their workplace is very or somewhat toxic. To ensure that we are working from the same definition, a toxic workplace is defined as harmful conditions that directly impact mental health. The following are some additional statistics from the 2023 APA Survey:

- Fifty-eight percent of people who report working in a toxic environment state that they have fair/poor mental health.
- Fifty-two percent of people who report working in a toxic environment state that they have experienced harm to their mental health at work.
- More females (23 percent) reported a toxic workplace than males (15 percent).
- More people living with a disability (26 percent) reported a toxic workplace than those without a disability (16 percent).
- Twenty-four percent of respondents said someone within or outside their organization had yelled at or verbally abused them at work within the past twelve months.
- Nineteen percent reported having experienced bullying at work.
- Twelve percent of manual laborers reported that someone within their organization displayed physical violence toward them, and 5 percent of office workers reported the same.

- Twenty-two percent of workers experienced harassment at work in the past twelve months.[40]

As much as I dream that one day we will be free from these hideous behaviors, the reality is that incivility is still alive and well in workplaces throughout America, and it's continuing to wreak havoc on people's mental health. I wrote an entire book, *Making Work Work*, on how to effectively navigate the challenges of workplace incivility, so I won't rehash all of that here. Instead, allow me to share a new idea with you.

If you are dealing with incivility at work, this simple mindset shift can be helpful. Ask yourself, "Are you operating from your standards or from your expectations?"

Standards versus Expectations

This distinction is an incredibly valuable tool in navigating relationships, whether they are professional or personal. Standards are objective, and they are about the level of quality that we live by and set for ourselves. Expectations are subjective, and they are ideas about how we want others or the world to be. Standards are fact based and are within our control, whereas expectations are fiction based and fall outside of our control.

Here is a personal example from my life: I have a standard of being treated with respect, but I don't *expect* others to treat me with respect. I know that sounds confusing, so please allow me to elaborate. Because of the two most traumatic experiences in my life (specifically, my sexual assault and suicide attempt), I have decided that being respected is crucial in any relationship that I've deemed

40 "2023 Work in America survey," https://www.apa.org/pubs/reports/work-in-america/2023-workplace-health-well-being.

important to me, so I make that standard clear to others. However, when someone treats me with disrespect (e.g., spreads rumors about me, ignores my boundaries, or insults me), I kindly restate my standard, and if it happens again, then I leave that relationship behind. Restating my standard of respect could simply look like this: "if there is something that you need to tell me, I would appreciate it if you told me directly instead of talking about me behind my back. Please don't do it again."

On the contrary, whenever I had an *expectation* that others should treat me with respect, I was putting the responsibility on them to behave accordingly. And if I'm being honest, I usually did so without clearly communicating my standards to them. Unfortunately, since people can't read my mind, I ended up feeling annoyed and frustrated when people did not meet the expectations that I held for them. As the best-selling author Anne Lamott wisely said, "Expectations are resentments waiting to happen." Truer words have never been spoken. To avoid this, I don't put the expectation that I'll be treated with respect on anyone. Instead, I come equipped with my standards and know that it's on me to communicate them clearly and, if necessary, to act accordingly.

What does that have to do with workplace civility? Quite a bit, actually. In my consulting work, I have run into hundreds of people who expect their colleagues and boss to treat them with kindness and civility. Almost every time, that is a recipe for disaster, and they find themselves consumed with frustration, anger, and resentment. But what if civility was a personal *standard* instead? If so, that could likely inspire you to show up differently.

Your Colleague <raised voice>: "Hey, what in the hell are you doing?! The meeting started five minutes ago. Get in the conference room!"

You: "Yes, I'm aware that I'm running late—I'm finishing up with a client, and I shared that with the team. More importantly, if you need me to do something, there's no need to raise your voice at me. Please don't do it again."

That response is firm, clear, and civil. Most important, you behaved in alignment with your standards of civility. Yes, this also works for supervisors.

Your Boss <angrily slams fist on table>: "This report does not meet my expectations! I can't present this to the board on Friday! What were you thinking submitting this to me?!"

You: "I'm sorry to hear that this report didn't meet your expectations. Can you provide specifics on where I fell short? I made a point to follow the outline that you gave me in our one-on-one meeting last week."

Your Boss: "I shouldn't have to hold your hand on this; you figure it out.[41] I have another meeting in five minutes—Leave!"

You: "OK. I'll work on it. Also, before I go—may I ask that you don't raise your voice or slam your fist on the table during our meetings? I'm happy to accept feedback, but that type of hostility makes me uncomfortable."

Your Boss: "Seriously?! I have every right to be pissed about this steaming donkey turd that you're calling a report. Grow up and get out."

41 *Sidenote: this approach is an example of the Burden of Proof logical fallacy from chapter 6.*

Sheesh, that didn't go well, did it? I know that it may seem that way, but appearances can be deceiving. In this situation with your boss, you stayed true to your standard of civility, which will serve you way more often than it won't. Similar to the response to your colleague, your response was calm, firm, respectful, and even helpful—you did try to get more information from your boss to revise your report, after all.

If you're thinking, "Yeah, there's no way that I'm talking to my boss like that." I have to ask: Like *what*, exactly? In this example, were you disrespectful? Rude? Insubordinate? No. Remember in chapter 3 when I mentioned the biggest myth about civility is that you must roll over and accept the horrors of the world with passive resignation and a lowered head? That serves no one. Civility includes the radical act of respectfully standing up for yourself, which, in this example, you did successfully.

Aligning with our standards is a simple way to reclaim our personal power instead of giving that power away by expecting others to behave in a certain way. Continuing with the prior scenario, what if your boss becomes more abusive? If you remain aligned to your standards, you can respectfully ask your boss again not to behave like that, and if your boss ignores you, escalate the issue to Human Resources or work diligently to find a work environment that meets your standards.

Personally speaking, after enduring a toxic workplace for nearly two years, I attempted suicide because I expected my colleagues to be kinder to me. In other words, my unmet expectations of others nearly killed me. Over twenty years later, I wonder how different things could have been if kindness and civility were the standards that guided my life instead of expecting other people to give me what I should have demanded for myself.

2. The Incivility of Intolerance

One of the things that I am asked about the most in my travels is how to deal with bias and microaggressions with civility. We've already covered implicit bias in chapter 6, but a microaggression, as defined by *Merriam-Webster*, is a comment or action that subtly, and often unconsciously or unintentionally, expresses a prejudiced attitude toward a member of a marginalized group.[42] Despite "micro" being a part of the word, please know that microaggressions play a large role in adding to the incivility of the world.

The word "microaggression" implies that these are small, and therefore, insignificant slights—or worse, it is a sign that people are becoming too sensitive by clutching to their victimhood. Nothing could be further from the truth. It could be argued that if these slights happened once, then, sure, you could brush it off and keep it moving. The problem with microaggressions is that they don't happen once, and the cumulative effect of them has been referred to as "death by a thousand papercuts." Personally speaking, having people hurriedly cross the street when they see me walking down the sidewalk, clutch their purses when I enter an elevator (or immediately jump off the elevator as if they were shot out of a circus cannon), assume that I'm capable only of uttering sentences with monosyllabic words, or being accused of theft in department stores has been a common occurrence in my life for decades, and it is truly exhausting.

Also, it's worth noting that everyone on earth, regardless of race, ethnicity, religion, or physical ability, is capable of delivering microaggression. If this book landed in the hands of someone who is interested in uniting our world around civility, then one of the steps in doing so

---

42 Merriam-Webster, "microaggression," https://www.merriam-webster.com/dictionary/microaggression.

is by raising our awareness to the soul-destroying impact of microaggressions and bias.

There are three challenging areas to address, and we'll do so with practical tips: the first is what to do if you commit a microaggression; second, what to do if you're the target of a microaggression; and lastly, what to do if you observe a microaggression.

If You Commit a Microaggression: Intent versus Impact

The following is a list of common microaggressions that I have collected over my years of professional training, coaching, and consulting work. It's not an exhaustive list, but I'm curious if any of these look familiar to you. And if not, ask yourself, if you would be OK with having to deal with these insensitive behaviors on a near-daily basis for the remainder of your life.

Actions

- Touching a Black person's hair or touching a pregnant woman's belly without permission
- Continually misusing a person's pronouns after the person has repeatedly shared their preferred pronoun with you
- A store employee following a person of color around the store because they assume that they are going to steal something
- Referring to a white doctor as "Dr. ______" but referring to a doctor of color by their first name
- Continually mispronouncing a person's name or making up a nickname for them that's easier for you to pronounce

- Consistently confusing people of the same racial group for one another
- Expecting a person of a marginalized group to be the "unofficial spokesperson" for that marginalized group

Words

- "You don't act Black/Gay/Latino/Jewish"
- "You speak English so well!" (Said with surprise to a non-white person)
- "Don't you miss being able to do ________?" (Said to a person with a disability)
- "What *are* you?"
- "Wearing a hat to work is unprofessional." (Said to a person wearing a religious head covering)
- "That's so gay" or "That's so retarded"
- "Why are you people always so loud and/or angry?"
- "I'm so OCD about how I clean my office."
- "When I see you, I don't see your race." (If you're unsure why this is problematic, I unpacked this fully in my previous book, *Go Together*)

It's possible that many of these are familiar to you, but you might also realize that you have done or said one or more of these, unintentionally. If you're like most folks (myself included), the reflexive response is to declare, "I didn't intend to be offensive; I didn't know better!" Fair enough, but does our intent really matter when we harm someone?

For example, say I'm running around my local neighborhood park wearing steel-toed work boots, and I carelessly step on the foot of a woman wearing open-toed shoes and break three of her toes. I clearly wasn't trying to disable her, but when she's writhing on the ground in pain, does it make sense to keep hammering her with "that wasn't my intent"? That may be true, but that doesn't change the objective reality (the impact) that she'll likely be in a walking boot for four to six weeks because of my actions, whether I intended to do it or not. Owning the impact of my actions is what matters in this moment, not irrelevant ramblings about my intent.

Case in point—years ago in a presentation, I used the word "lame" repeatedly to describe something that was low-quality and undesirable. In front of everyone in attendance, one of the audience members kindly and firmly mentioned that "lame" was a flippant term to describe a person with a disability, and she was offended by my repeated use of it. The last thing that I was trying to do was offend anyone or make fun of people with disabilities, and initially, I wanted to get defensive and focus on the purity of my intentions. Thankfully, I summoned the impulse control not to do that.

If you are interested in increasing the civility in our world after committing a microaggression, here are some things to do and not do:

- *Do*: Reflect on the impact of your words and/or actions.
- *Do*: Own it and sincerely apologize. ("I'm sorry that I made that comment, and I understand how it was hurtful.")
- *Do*: Acknowledge your impact and commit to do better, going forward.
- *Don't*: Say "I'm sorry that you were offended."
- *Don't*: Say "I'm sorry if I said something to upset you." ("Ifs" and "buts" should be nowhere near a sincere apology.)
- *Don't*: Reiterate your intent and make it about you.

After I made my unfortunate "lame" comment, I sincerely apologized, fully owned my ignorance about the meaning of the word, and pledged to do better, going forward. It ended up being a powerful learning moment for me and, from what I heard afterward, for others in the audience who witnessed it.

However, there were some people in the audience who thought that my apology was unnecessary. One man said to me afterward, "So wait a minute, are you saying that I need to apologize every time someone gets offended by something that I did or said, innocently? When does it become the responsibility of the other person to grow up, get some thicker skin, and quit being victimized by everything that makes them uncomfortable? This nonsense is getting out of hand."

The gentleman and I saw the situation differently. The way I see it, who am I to judge why someone is offended by what I said or did? If I'm trying to create a more civil world, it costs me nothing to ask questions to better understand the impact of my words or actions, own the fact that I may have harmed someone, and commit to do better.

That also leads me to a related point—some people have said to me, "I'm so afraid of saying the wrong thing and offending people, so I feel like it's safest to be quiet so I won't get canceled." Spoiler alert, my friend: if you're serious about engaging in this work, you *will* say the wrong thing, just as I did and, unfortunately, will likely continue to do. We can't afford to have anyone opt out of this important work because of fear of the inevitable mistake. The expectation that you need to throw a perfect game every time you step on the pitcher's mound is unreasonable and exhausting. All that is required is to do the best you can, when you make a mistake, own it, and then course-correct going forward.

If You Are the Target of a Microaggression: The Question

Many people who are on the receiving end of microaggressions don't know how to respond in a way that doesn't make the situation worse. Not to mention, when you're hit with a microaggression, you are forced into an uncomfortable space where you must immediately answer a series of yes-or-no questions, within seconds:

- "Should I address this now?"
- "Should I address this later?"
- "Should I let it go?"
- "Do I have a relationship worth maintaining with this person?"
- "Am I trying to raise awareness that what they did or said is problematic?"
- "Am I hoping to change their behavior?"
- "Am I trying to honor myself?"

And to make this even more challenging, each answer presents a choose-your-own-adventure of consequences that could affect your career, your reputation, your self-worth, and your mental health. In an attempt to make this impossibly complex situation a little simpler, there's a six-word question that you can ask when someone directs a microaggression your way. It's the same one that I used with the driver in the beginning of this chapter.

"What do you mean by that?"

This question is gold when dealing with an ignorant statement because the person who said it is now forced to unpack and explain the bias behind what they said. Continuing the story from the beginning of this chapter, here's how it went down with the driver on the car ride to the airport:

Driver: "Why can't more Black folks be polite like you?"

Me: "What do you mean by that?"

Driver <becoming flustered>: "Um … uh … that didn't come out right. I should have just complimented you without saying that."

Me: "Fair enough, but I hope that you don't believe that Black folks aren't polite, because you're too smart of a guy to think something like that. I'm sure we both agree that there are polite and impolite people of all races, right?"

Driver: "Yes sir, that was a stupid thing to say, and I'm sorry."

My friend, whom I'll call Racquel, had a similar encounter. She is in a same-sex marriage, and this is how she described her recent encounter at an auto dealership.

Racquel: "Thank you for your help! I'll have my wife pick up the car tomorrow afternoon once she gets off from work."

Sales Representative <shocked>: "Wait … you're a lesbian? But you're so pretty!"

Racquel: "What do you mean by that?"

Sales Representative: "Um … I meant that I've never seen a lesbian who looks like you before."

Racquel: "I appreciate being called pretty, and there are a lot of women who are beautiful whether they are straight, gay, or otherwise. I hope that you weren't implying that all lesbians are ugly."

Sales Representative <sheepishly>: "No, of course not. I don't know why I even said that."

In both cases, it's like my driver and Racquel's sales representative metaphorically tried to give us a gift package. Unfortunately, the "gift" was a booby-trapped box packed with sticky green slime ready to explode all over the person who opened it. Instead of us opening the package and being covered in goo, we figuratively said, "No thanks, you go ahead and open it and tell us what's inside." At that point, they were the ones who were forced to navigate their way out of the mess they created, not us. The "what do you mean by that?" question is a great way to increase others' self-awareness by having them unpack their problematic remarks, without you having to donate your emotional labor for their benefit.

On the contrary, if the microaggression is an *action* instead of something that was said, responding by asking "What do you mean by that?" obviously wouldn't make any sense. In these situations involving a problematic action, a simple, clear, and firm correction in the moment may be enough. Let's revisit the list from earlier in the chapter, with potential solutions.

- Someone reaches for your pregnant belly; response: "please don't touch my belly, it makes me uncomfortable."
- Continually misusing a person's pronouns after the person has repeatedly shared their preferred pronoun with you; response:

"my pronouns are she/her. Is there anything that I can do to help you to remember this?"

- Store employee following a person of color around the store because they assume that they are going to steal something; response: "I see you over there. I'm just browsing, in case you were wondering."
- Referring to a white doctor as "Dr. _____" but referring to a doctor of color by their first name; response: "It's Dr. Ramirez, not Julia."
- Continually mispronouncing a person's name, or making up a nickname for them that's easier for you to pronounce; response: "My name is Olufemi, not 'Ollie.' If you need help with the phonetic pronunciation, I'm happy to help."
- Consistently confusing people of the same racial group for one another; response: "I'm not Hiromi, I'm Jade. I'm concerned why you keep mixing the two of us up."
- Expecting a person of a marginalized group to be the "unofficial spokesperson" for that marginalized group; response: "Thank you for the offer, but I don't want to be the chair of the LGBTQ Committee just because I'm gay."

Again, all of these are firm, respectful, and civil. You don't have to accept bad behavior. Also, as a final point on this—not everything is deserving of your finite emotional energy. Sometimes, the best thing that you can do is brush it off, protect your peace, and not give the person the benefit of your thoughts, feelings, and time. As always, this decision is up to your discretion.

If You Observe a Microaggression: Be an Upstander

Lastly, if you happen to observe someone else become the target of microaggression, one of the ways that you can make the situation better is by becoming an upstander. Being an upstander is commonly associated with bullying prevention, but the premise behind it works for interrupting microaggressions as well. An upstander is someone who chooses to support a person who is being abused or harmed.[43] It's the opposite of being a bystander, which brings no value when it comes to creating a more civil world.

Early on in my professional career, I remember going to a meeting that was attended by mostly men and only one woman, whom I'll call Joan. It was a brainstorming session, and Joan shared an idea that sounded clever and useful. The men in the group barely acknowledged her contribution to the discussion and quickly moved on to gather more suggestions. No less than five minutes later, a man in the meeting repeated the *exact same idea* that Joan said, almost verbatim. Many of the men in the room stopped in their tracks to praise the brilliance of this idea and almost unanimously agreed to apply it immediately. Joan looked deflated, until another man at the meeting interrupted the celebratory back-patting to share what should have been an obvious observation. "I noticed that Joan made that exact same suggestion a few minutes earlier, and no one acknowledged it. In my opinion, if anyone should be getting the credit for this idea, it's her." It was a beautiful moment, and Joan pulled the man aside in the hallway afterward to let him know how much she appreciated it.

Being an upstander doesn't come without its pitfalls, and just like anything, it could be done poorly and make the situation worse. One simple rule is not to speak for another person. For example, if someone

---

43 "How to be an upstander," https://www.esafety.gov.au/young-people/be-an-upstander.

made an inappropriate comment about people with disabilities, and unbeknownst to them, a person with a disability was in the room to hear it, please for the love of all things kind, civil, and positive, don't do this. "Hey! That comment is inappropriate and offensive to Rick! Can't you see that he's sitting right there? Apologize to him right now!" *Oh man.* An uncomfortable situation just became unbearable in a hurry, and now poor Rick probably wants to hide from the world like the centerpiece in a Russian nesting doll set. Instead of speaking for Rick, we can simply speak for ourselves. "Hey, I find that comment to be offensive, and it's not OK." There is no need to be anyone's savior.

In addition, if you lean toward being nonconfrontational in your approach, you can still be a very effective upstander. If you noticed that a person is upset by something that someone said, a powerful way to be helpful is to check in with the target after the fact. Lending an empathetic ear or a kind word of encouragement can go a long way in helping the targeted person regain their faith in the goodness of humanity.

Final point on microaggressions and bias—I urge you to avoid the tempting and often lazy bait of *immediately* labeling someone a racist, anti-Semite, homophobe, or misogynist whenever someone says or does something offensive. As mentioned in the previous chapter, the Boomerang Effect will ensure that the only thing you will achieve is the person becoming defensive, or worse, becoming more entrenched in their problematic views. By focusing on the person's behavior ("I found what you said to be offensive") instead of focusing on the person ("you're a racist"), the door can remain open for learning, growth, and ideally positive change.

The Incivility of Radicalization

The third most common concern that I've heard is about dealing with people who have become radicalized. According to the United Nations Office on Drugs and Crime, radicalization occurs when an individual adopts an increasingly extremist set of beliefs and aspirations.[44] More so than ever, people have reached out to me fearing that friends and loved ones are becoming susceptible to radical ideas, so we need to be aware of it, ideally before it happens.

There are some clear warning signs to look out for:

Isolation from Prior Relationships: The person withdraws from relationships and social activities that they once enjoyed. Once healthy connections with friends, family, colleagues, or social activities that were a central part of their lives, are no longer of interest to them.

Behavior Change and Hostile Attitude: The person openly expresses anger, resentment, or hostility toward a specific group of people and, in some cases, communicates a desire to cause them harm. They also can become angry when presented with alternative viewpoints.

Online Obsession: A person spends the majority of their time intensely engaged with an online community, sharing problematic content on social media, and being singularly focused on being around people who share similar radical beliefs and ideologies.

The *Current Opinion in Psychology* article "Terrorism, Radicalization and De-Radicalization" introduced three phases of radicalization:

The Sensitivity Phase: Often driven by feelings of insignificance. Whether it's caused by a loss of status, a strong sense of humiliation, poor career prospects, or the idea that another group is responsible for their discontent.

44 UNODC, "'Radicalization' and 'violent extremism,'" https://www.unodc.org/e4j/en/terrorism/module-2/key-issues/radicalization-violent-extremism.html.

The Group Membership Phase: The individual joins a group of like-minded people and adopts the norms and values of the group to strengthen the commitment to the cause.

The Action Phase: People turn to using violence against others.[45]

People aren't born as radicals or extremists. It's a process that can happen slowly and steadily over time. Unquestionably, the best way to deal with radicalization is to prevent it from occurring in the first place, and many of the ICIs in this book up to this point were written to assist in that important effort. Unfortunately, it is possible that you are reading this book with the sobering realization that someone you care about has already become radicalized and prevention is no longer an option. If that's the case, then the effort to help them may be some of the hardest work you have ever done.

Addressing Radicalization: Radical Civility

In my travels, I'm often asked a variation of these questions: "How can I be civil to people who traffic in unhinged conspiracy theories? If I believe that two plus two equals four, and they believe that two plus two equals Tuesday, how can we ever find common ground if we don't share the basic foundation of reality?"

Those are fair questions. As I navigate situations with people who share with me that their loved one has been radicalized, I remind them of this simple truth: most bad behaviors are an unskilled expression of an unmet need.

Many people who approach me about radicalized individuals in their lives do so with a sense of exasperation and anger at their

45 Bertjan Doosje, Fathali M. Moghaddam, Arie W. Kruglanski, Arjan de Wolf, Liesbeth Mann, Allard R. Feddes, "Terrorism, Radicalization and De-radicalization," Current Opinion in Psychology 11, (2016): 79–84. https://www.sciencedirect.com/science/article/abs/pii/S2352250X16300811.

inability to see the truth. What if we change the way that we look at folks who have succumbed to the pull of radicalization? What if we realized that their behavior was an expression of an unmet need? Embracing this perspective could change everything.

In many cases, people who have become radicalized are deeply unhappy and have been led to believe that someone else is the cause of their unhappiness. Because of this, they have a need to feel in control of their lives, a need to feel significant, a need for justice, a need to belong, or a need to feel good about themselves. If they can't skillfully find a way to address those needs in an appropriate manner that doesn't harm anyone, then it is clear to see how a person may be drawn toward less-skilled means of getting their needs met. Most important, remember this truth: somehow and in some way, being part of a radicalized community is fulfilling a need that is missing from your loved one's life.

While not a completely seamless comparison, there are a lot of similarities between a person who has been radicalized and a person suffering from substance addiction:

- Both may begin with a desire to soothe an unmet need, and the behavior can escalate over time to continue to have the need met.
- Both behaviors can become reinforced by people in their social networks who share an interest in the same behaviors.
- In both cases, healing cannot begin until there is a firm realization that they have a problem.
- Both likely won't respond favorably to being shamed, humiliated, or spoken to in a condescending manner. If anything, that will deepen their problematic behaviors.

So, what can we do? We can offer civility. Specifically, an active demonstration of respect and the ability to disagree without disrespect.

To be painfully clear, I am *not* expecting you to offer civility to a radicalized person who you don't know or care about. I realize that may be a bridge too far, so I won't insult you or embarrass myself by suggesting it. I will reiterate an earlier suggestion though: save your efforts by not wasting time attacking them for their beliefs, because that won't do anything except make the problem worse. Many radicalized people are actively looking for a fight, so by calling them stupid, unhinged, or crazy, not only are you playing directly into their hands, but you're also adding gasoline to the fire that you are trying to extinguish. Second, whether it's someone you care about or not, I'm not suggesting that you should ignore or make excuses for behaviors that could put them, you, or others at risk. If you're concerned, separate yourself from them without apology, and if necessary, tell others—teachers, parents, or the authorities—who can take proper action to prevent a potentially catastrophic escalation.

With that said, if this *is* a person you care about, then civility—or, as I'll call it in this case, *radical civility*—is the only answer.

It's radical because it's an uncommon approach that most people won't find the willingness to put into action. Choosing to show the radicalized person respect by listening with an open mind, giving them compassion and kindness, and not disrespecting them for their beliefs can become a means for the person to have their needs met in a healthy way. The goal of creating this space is to show the person that they have value as a human being, without needing to retreat to an extremist group in order to feel valued. As hard as this sounds, this is the most effective means of rescuing someone who is consumed by radical ideologies. Contrary to popular belief, this doesn't mean that you need a shred of respect for any of their beliefs or even to pretend that you do. But, by offering a space to show *the person* respect—the respect they crave but are likely not receiving—it can potentially open the door for alternative viewpoints, self-awareness, and healing.

No one knows this better than Tony McAleer. Tony is the author of the book, *The Cure for Hate: A Former White Supremacist's Journey from Violent Extremism to Radical Compassion*. As the title of his book indicates, Tony spent fifteen years deeply entrenched in the white nationalist movement, even rising up in the ranks as a leader who actively contributed to the spread of propaganda, hate, and violence in his community and beyond. He is now the cofounder of Life after Hate, a nonprofit organization. Its mission is to build a safer society by making it possible for people to break free from lives of violent hate and extremism through evidence-based interventions.[46]

How did Tony go from being deeply radicalized to being on the forefront of healing people who are entrenched in extremist ideologies? For him, it began with the birth of his daughter, followed by the birth of his son fifteen months later. As he began to receive positive attention in his role as a single father, his unmet need of being seen and appreciated was finally being met in a healthy way. This shift in his identity also inspired him to clearly view the white supremacist movement, in his words, as, "completely dysfunctional. Wounded people, alcoholism, violence. I can't think of a single person who experienced joy on a daily basis."[47]

In addition, as Tony began to slowly move away from the extremist ideologies, he encountered a leadership trainer and speaker named Dov Baron, whom Tony now credits as a mentor. In an early encounter between the two of them, Tony shared his past life as a

46 https://www.lifeafterhate.org/about-us/.

47 Jason Wlson, "Life after white supremacy: the former neo-fascist now working to fight hate," April 4, 2017, https://www.theguardian.com/world/2017/apr/04/life-after-hate-groups-neo-fascism-racism.

white supremacist, and a transformative moment happened immediately afterward. Dov smiled at Tony and surprisingly revealed, "Tony, you do realize that I'm a Jew, right?"

Dov recalled, "It was clear to me as we were talking about it that he's out of the movement, but the movement is not out of him. He was full of piss and vinegar. A bright guy, but it was all misdirected because of his own shit, the same as all of us. I told him 'that's not who you are. That's what you did, but that's not who you are. *I see you.*'" That is when Tony broke down and cried.[48]

We all want to be seen. We all want to be respected. We all want to be connected to others. Unfortunately, some people choose maladaptive—and in some cases, violent—means to get those desires met. However, if we can see past the hardened exterior of the radicalized person, hopefully we can effectively see the truth: the person in front of us is someone who is searching for meaningful human connection. As mentioned, rescuing someone from the grip of radicalization is not for the faint of heart, but if you are willing to provide that meaningful connection through civility, your actions could be the spark that saves a life.

Dr. Martin Luther King Jr. wisely said in one of his most famous sermons, *Loving Your Enemies*:

> Returning hate for hate multiplies hate, adding deeper darkness to a night already devoid of stars. Darkness cannot drive out darkness, only light can do that. Hate cannot drive out hate, only love can do that.

In a world that defaults to fighting hate with hate, it is a radical act to respond with love, kindness, and civility when most lack the stamina, courage, or interest to do so.

---

48 Ibid.

INTENTIONAL CONSISTENT INTERVENTION #21: *STANDARDS VERSUS EXPECTATIONS*

Understanding the critical difference between our standards and our expectations can play a significant role in reducing unproductive disagreements and resentments.

ICI Steps:

1. Review the difference between standards and expectations on pages 213-216.
2. In your *Civil Unity Journal*, list your top three standards that will guide your life. Review this list on a daily basis, and feel free to modify it, whenever necessary.
3. Also in your *Civil Unity Journal*, list out the expectations that you currently hold for people.
4. Ask yourself, "How will I commit to releasing those expectations and focus on my three standards?" Write your answer in your *Civil Unity Journal*.
5. In your *Civil Unity Journal*, write down how to communicate your standards clearly and respectfully to others.

INTENTIONAL CONSISTENT INTERVENTION #22: *IMPACT VERSUS INTENT*

When you make a mistake and harm someone with your words or your actions (and since you're human, you will), ensure that you are focused primarily on your impact, not your intention.

ICI Steps:

1. Whenever you harm someone unintentionally, sincerely apologize, own your part in the harmful impact, and commit to doing better, going forward.
2. Do not focus on your intentions and make the situation about yourself. If you find yourself doing this, shift the conversation back to your impact and step 1 of this ICI.
3. In your *Civil Unity Journal*, document the situation and answer the following questions: "Was I able to stay focused on my impact, or did I shift the conversation back to my intent? When I focused on my impact, did it make a positive difference in the quality of the conversation?"

INTENTIONAL CONSISTENT INTERVENTION #23: *WHAT DO YOU MEAN BY THAT?*

If you find yourself in a situation where someone has said something upsetting or problematic to you, you don't have to own all of the discomfort.

ICI Steps:

1. When someone says something to you that is clearly offensive and inappropriate, put them in the position to explain themselves by asking, "What do you mean by that?"
2. If the person becomes self-aware about the problematic comment, use that opportunity to reiterate in your own words why you found it to be offensive.
3. If the "what do you mean by that?" question does not inspire any self-awareness (or worse, they double

down on their comment), decide if you want to expend the emotional labor to educate them about why their comment was harmful. It is always OK to choose not to engage any further.

4. In your *Civil Unity Journal*, document this experience fully. Describe the offensive comment, the person's response to the "what do you mean by that?" question, and whether it contributed to the other person's learning and growth.

INTENTIONAL CONSISTENT INTERVENTION #24: *BE AN UPSTANDER*

If you observe microaggression or bias, commit to being an upstander.

ICI Steps:

1. When you observe microaggression or bias, decide if it would be appropriate to speak up in the moment or later. This is more art than science, meaning that you will need to be able to effectively read the room. Acknowledge and accept that you will not get this right 100 percent of the time. Most important, commit to the idea that in order to build a more civil world, being a bystander is not an option.
2. When you choose to speak up, please do not speak for the targeted party. Speak only for yourself.
3. In your *Civil Unity Journal*, document the situation, what you said as an upstander, whether you said it in

the moment or later, and if your intervention had any positive effect on the situation.

INTENTIONAL CONSISTENT INTERVENTION #25: *RADICAL CIVILITY*

It is a radical act to offer civility—namely, an active demonstration of respect and the willingness to disagree without disrespect—to a loved one who has been radicalized.

ICI Steps:

1. Review the warning signs of radicalization on pages 228-229.
2. If you have determined that your loved one is at risk of becoming radicalized (or already is), resist the urge to respond with judgment, condescension, and disrespect. Instead, listen to the person, show respect (not necessarily for their views but for the person), and remember that their behavior is likely an unskilled expression of an unmet need. In your *Civil Unity Journal*, write down what you believe is your loved one's unmet need.
3. In your *Civil Unity Journal*, describe what it was like to actively listen and show respect to the loved one who has been radicalized. This is extremely difficult work, and it's work that most people cannot, or will not, do (and since this is an ICI, you will need to do this consistently). Ask yourself, "Did actively listening and showing respect to your loved one make any positive difference in your opinion? Why or why not?"

CHAPTER 9

When Civility Feels Impossible

To forgive is to set a prisoner free
and discover that the prisoner was you.

—LEWIS B. SMEDES

This final chapter was the hardest one for me to write.

On the one hand, I passionately believe that civility is the force that can unite our society. As discussed in previous chapters, civility practically applied can make a positive difference when dealing with workplace incivility, intolerance, divisive issues, people who traffic in misinformation or disinformation, and even with folks who have been radicalized.

On the other hand, even though rage, disrespect, polarization, and middle-finger discourse have failed us spectacularly in society, I can understand and empathize with anyone who defaults to these as their go-to strategies. As mentioned in chapter 1, I was forced into a sexual act with two older boys when I was a child. Shortly after college, I walked in on my longtime girlfriend (who I thought I was going to marry) having sex with one of my friends. Decades ago, I worked in a toxic environment full of sociopathic bullies, and I believed that the only escape was to take my own life.

None of this makes me special, mind you. I have known people who have endured the worst that life has to offer. A family losing their only child because of the carelessness of a drunk driver. A woman whose husband cheated on her for years and eventually infected her with an incurable sexually transmitted disease. A businessman whose business partner—who was also his lifelong friend—betrayed him by stealing all of the company's money, destroying his life's work, and leaving him bankrupt. The number of heartbreaking stories where a person has been hurt physically, emotionally, financially, mentally, and spiritually by another person are too numerous to mention in this book.

There is no doubt that you also have been harmed physically or emotionally, have had your trust broken, or have been treated in an inexcusable manner in your lifetime. I don't think that people are drawn to a book about civility because they have lived a charmed life where no one treated them poorly. I can't speak for you—but if you're anything like me—at the time of the transgression, I would have rather bathed in a tub full of rabid possums than offer civility to the perpetrators.

That's why the human experience is so complicated. We can logically and rationally understand that civility is a sound strategy, but when strong emotions are introduced into the mix, all of our best laid plans turn into vapor. In my travels, the most common questions I receive about offering civility in difficult circumstances are, "Is it possible to be civil to someone who has deeply hurt me? And, should I be civil to them?"

This is the hardest part of the civility journey, so I saved it for last. And it all comes down to one of the most powerful and often misunderstood acts in human behavior: forgiveness.

Forgiveness: Debunking Myths and Difficult Questions

It is fascinating to me that almost any broken bone in our bodies will heal within the span of a few months at the longest, but the injury of broken trust may not heal over a lifetime. Forgiveness is the most effective balm to expedite emotional healing.

Generally speaking, forgiveness is an intentional decision to let go of resentment, vengeance, and anger toward a person or group who has harmed you. It is not hyperbole to say that forgiveness not only can expedite emotional healing, but it could also save your life. According to Johns Hopkins Medicine, people who are more forgiving tend to be more satisfied with their lives and have less depression, anxiety, stress, anger, and hostility. Conversely, people who hold on to grudges are more likely to experience severe depression, PTSD, as well as other health conditions.[49] This supports the iconic quote, often misattributed to Buddha, "Holding a grudge is like drinking poison and expecting the other person to die."

At baseline, remember this—forgiveness is *not* a gift to the person who harmed you. Forgiveness is a life-saving gift to yourself to release the burden of holding on to anger so that you can regain your emotional health and peace of mind. So, if forgiveness is such a powerful force for healing, why don't people forgive more often? That's a fair question, and it will require us to correct five widely held beliefs about forgiveness:

1. *Forgiveness does not mean condoning what happened to you.* From what I've seen with my professional and personal connections, this is the primary reason why people choose not to forgive others. I cannot say this firmly enough: what happened to you was not OK, and you never have to—and it could be argued that you shouldn't—reach a point in your lifetime where you are fine with what happened to you.

2. *Forgiveness is not about absolving the person of accountability.* The act of forgiveness has nothing to do with freeing people from accountability for their harmful actions. You can forgive someone and still hold them accountable by permanently removing them from your life or even testifying against them in a court of law, if necessary.

3. *Forgiveness is not a demonstration of weakness.* The belief that forgiveness is a sign of weakness is flat out wrong, and nothing could be further from the truth. The ability to consciously

49 "Forgiveness: your health depends on it," https://www.hopkinsmedicine.org/health/wellness-and-prevention/forgiveness-your-health-depends-on-it.

and intentionally release negative feelings after being harmed takes not only an immense amount of strength but courage as well. It is far easier to cling to anger and bitterness instead of engaging in the excruciating labor of working through those unpleasant emotions to release their vice grip on our lives. Mahatma Gandhi says it best: "The weak can never forgive. Forgiveness is the attribute of the strong."

4. *Forgiveness does not require reconciliation.* There are cases when forgiveness sets the groundwork to resume the relationship, which is fine if that's what you choose. However, forgiveness doesn't mean that you have to pick up the relationship where you left off. You may decide that you are ready to forgive someone while simultaneously deciding that you want to maintain healthy boundaries by keeping that person out of your life.

5. *Forgiveness is not a one-time act.* This is something that I used to believe, but it's not true. What I now know for sure is that simply declaring, "I forgive the person who harmed me," will not be enough. If you have been deeply hurt, it will likely take time to process your feelings, understand how deeply you've been harmed, and decide how you can move forward. Also, if you decided to reconcile with the person who harmed you, it will take a significant amount of time to rebuild the trust that has been broken in your relationship. Not to mention, just when you thought that you have emotionally moved past your pain, something could retrigger you, reopen old wounds, and put you right back where you started. In other words, the act of forgiveness is more like a dial than a switch.

Understanding the truth about forgiveness is an important step in building a civil society. Since everyone has been hurt by another person, if we cling tightly to our pain (which, again, is an understandable response), it will be harder for us to come together. I've compiled the most challenging questions that I have received over the years in response to embracing the power of forgiveness and summarized them into four questions. I'll spend the remainder of the chapter answering them:

1. "Is it possible to forgive and forget?"
2. "Should I forgive someone who isn't sorry for what they did?"
3. "What if I can't forgive myself for what happened?"
4. "Is anything unforgivable?"

Let's dive in.

1. "Is It Possible to Forgive and Forget?"

Growing up, I heard the saying "forgive and forget" from teachers, spiritual leaders, and other well-meaning adults as a way to move forward after someone harms us. The suggestion is that you should not only forgive the person for hurting you, but also you should forget that they ever hurt you in the first place. Understandably, this is a controversial stance. Is it really a good thing to forgive and forget?

In the 2015 study, *Forgive and Forget: Differences between Decisional and Emotional Forgiveness*, the researchers made an important distinction between the two forms of forgiveness noted in the study's title.[50]

---

50 Stephanie Lichtenfeld, Vanessa L. Buechner, Markus A. Maier, Maria Fernández-Capo, "Forgive and Forget: Differences between Decisional and Emotional Forgiveness," *PLoS One* 10, no. 5: e0125561. https://www.ncbi.nlm.nih.gov/pmc/articles/PMC4422736/.

Decisional Forgiveness: An intentional decision to release feelings of anger, resentment, and vengeance by leaving them in the past and moving forward free from those feelings.

Emotional Forgiveness: The replacement of negative, unforgiving emotions with positive, other-oriented ones, such as empathy, compassion, or the willingness to understand.

Up to this point, we've primarily discussed decisional forgiveness. In this study, the researchers concluded that emotional forgiveness often leads to higher levels of forgetting than decisional forgiveness or no forgiveness. Now that the distinction is clear, let's return back to the earlier question: Is it really a good thing to forgive and forget?

Like with most difficult questions, it depends. From my personal experience, and similar to the study's findings, it has been easier to forget when I engaged in emotional forgiveness. I was recently in a car accident where another driver carelessly slammed into me after making an illegal U-turn, which destroyed my car and left me with minor injuries. As scary as that incident was, with time, I was able to replace my initial feelings of anger with feelings of empathy for the driver. Admittedly, it was easier for me to reach that point because the driver immediately expressed sincere remorse for his carelessness and I wasn't seriously injured. As I reflect back on the situations where I have reached a place of emotional forgiveness and, ultimately, forgetting, those moments have been easier with lower-stakes situations, relatively speaking.

However, if you are reading this as a survivor of trauma or abuse, that's an entirely different story. Anyone who has experienced a deeply traumatic episode, or trauma that occurred repeatedly over a period of time, is acutely aware that forgetting about what happened to them is a nearly impossible act. Not to mention, I can't even imagine what it would take for a trauma survivor to replace anger and vengeance with compassion or empathy for the person who harmed them. Personally speaking, I know that I haven't reached that point with the trauma that I have experienced, and I don't know if I'll ever get there (or if I even want to get there).

In those cases, it doesn't make sense to forgive and forget. Healing from trauma often involves the messy, emotional, and difficult process of examining the trauma to create appropriate coping strategies, and forgetting gets in the way of that. On the contrary, whether it's with a therapist, a support group, or a trusted friend, choosing to release negative emotions (decisional forgiveness) while also remembering the painful lessons can ensure that we retain the learning and possibly help others to avoid a similar fate.

2. "Is It Possible to Forgive Someone Who Isn't Sorry for What They Did?"

In early 2018, disgraced former USA Gymnastics and Michigan State doctor Larry Nassar was held accountable for the repeated sexual assault of hundreds of women and girls under his care (156 of them courageously gave emotional impact statements against him). Nassar is widely considered one of the most depraved sexual abusers who has ever walked the earth, and it is almost incomprehensible to quantify the depth and breadth of damage and pain that he caused during his career. Thankfully, he was later convicted for his numerous crimes and sentenced up to 175 years in prison. Despite Nassar bringing a Bible to the courtroom during the early hearings and speaking about praying for forgiveness, and even offering an apology in court, Judge Rosemarie Aquilina who presided over the case wasn't having any of it. Before delivering her sentence, Judge Aquilina read aloud a letter that Nassar wrote to the court that exposed his insincerity. Specifically in this letter, he defended his treatments and implied that the women who testified against him were lying.

"I was a good doctor because my treatments worked, and those patients that are now speaking out are the same ones that praised and came back over and over," Nassar wrote. "The media convinced them that everything I did was wrong and bad. They feel I broke their trust. Hell hath no fury like a woman scorned."

"I find that you don't get it, that you're a danger. That you remain a danger," Judge Aquilina said and later dismissively tossed the letter. She then added, "I wouldn't send my dogs to you, sir."[51]

Even if Larry Nassar delivered a sincere and heartfelt apology to the women and girls he abused with his monstrous behavior, I can't imagine a universe where that would be sufficient. *But he couldn't even do that.* Still though, some of the survivors of his abuse found the ability to forgive him.

Rachael Denhollander, a former gymnast and current attorney and author, was one of the survivors of Nassar's abuse. She was the first woman to pursue criminal charges and speak publicly against his criminality, and her tireless efforts were instrumental in his life imprisonment. In the courtroom, Rachael delivered an impassioned thirty-six-minute impact statement that was a masterclass in grace, strength, and courage. In her statement, and to the surprise of some, she mentioned that she forgave Nassar.

"I pray you experience the soul crushing weight of guilt so you may someday experience true repentance and true forgiveness from

---

51 Eric Levenson, "Larry Nassar sentenced to up to 175 years in prison for decades of sexual abuse," January 24, 2018. https://www.cnn.com/2018/01/24/us/larry-nassar-sentencing/index.html.

God, which you need far more than forgiveness from me—though I extend that to you as well."[52]

As Rachael showed, forgiveness is possible, even if the person who harmed you doesn't admit fault or apologize. She didn't wish for his well-being in prison or extend kindness to him, because the forgiveness she extended to him didn't require her to do either. The gift of forgiveness was one that she gave to herself so she could release the bitterness and move on with her life. That decision allowed her to positively impact countless lives with her work and advocacy, and it's doubtful that would have been possible if she was consumed with vengeance, which would be completely understandable.

There may be times when we are faced with extending forgiveness to someone who doesn't offer us an apology. The unfaithful spouse who left you for someone else, and they happily parade their newfound love all over social media. The morally casual salesperson who scammed you out of your life savings with false promises and continues to do it to others. The parent who ruled the household with a toxic blend of fear and abuse, who is now dead and unable to offer the apology that probably wouldn't have come anyway.

In those moments, finding the ability to release the feelings of anger toward them—whether it's through journaling, therapy, meditation, prayer, or other means—can be the act that saves our lives.

3. "What If I Can't Forgive Myself for What Happened?"

Out of the four questions, I believe this is the hardest one of all.

---

52 "Read Rachael Denhollander's full victim impact statement about Larry Nassar," January 30, 2018, https://www.cnn.com/2018/01/24/us/rachael-denhollander-full-statement/index.html.

As terrible as it is when someone else harms us, there are usually actions we can take to protect ourselves from being exposed to future harm. It becomes very complicated when we must sit with the sobering truth that we are the ones responsible for the harm caused to another person or to ourselves. A person falls asleep at the wheel while driving and severely injures an unsuspecting motorist. A student who is one semester away from graduating from college is caught cheating on their final exam and is expelled from school. A parent repeatedly dismissed their child's signs of depression as normal teenage moodiness, which later ends with the child dying by suicide.

Unlike the trauma caused by another person where we may be rightfully consumed with vengeance toward them, that's not possible when we are the ones who are responsible for the pain we're experiencing. The feelings of vengeance are turned inward and often present in one of two ways: guilt or shame.

Guilt is the awareness that *we did* something undesirable, wrong, or in violation of our values. Typically, it is associated with a specific action:

- "I lied to my spouse about meeting my ex for lunch."
- "I lost control and yelled at my assistant for no reason."
- "I broke my diet and ate two Big Macs for dinner."
- "I made a joke at a party that hurt the feelings of my friend."

Shame is a feeling that *we are* undesirable or wrong, which may or may not be in relation to an event or action:

- "I am a dishonest person who is undeserving of my spouse's love."
- "I am an awful boss who is incapable of leading anyone."

- "I am a pig with no self-control who is destined to be fat for the rest of my life."
- "I am a terrible person who keeps hurting the people in my life who are kind to me."

The simplest way to differentiate between guilt and shame is that guilt is typically focused on an action or behavior, whereas shame is typically focused on our worth as human beings. Guilt is an important emotion that allows us to acknowledge our mistakes and how our actions may have harmed someone or ourselves. Shame takes guilt to an unhealthy extreme. We may acknowledge the mistakes and own our part in it, but instead of it being a source of learning and self-improvement, it is used as a weapon of self-flagellation to validate our unworthiness as a person, which serves no one.

Returning back to the extreme examples that I mentioned in the beginning of this section, if a person severely injured a motorist, got expelled from school, or believes that they contributed to the suicide of their child, it's guilt—not shame—that has the power to inspire restorative action within us. Oftentimes, that restorative action is prompted by a deeper emotional expression of guilt, known as remorse. Guilt often says, "I did a bad thing." Shame says, "I am a bad person." And Remorse says, "I am very sorry for what I did, and I want to make amends." Theoretically, it's possible to feel guilt without remorse, and because of this, we must dig deeper than experiencing guilt or shame if we are serious about engaging in reparative action and atonement.

All of this leads us here: in order to reach self-forgiveness, it cannot happen without self-compassion. Self-compassion is the acknowledgment that we're all fallible human beings capable of mistakes, and in those instances, we must offer kindness to ourselves to reduce our suffering. The simplest way that I remind myself of this when I'm struggling to forgive myself for a harmful mistake is to ask this simple question: "If the person I loved the most made a similar mistake, would I talk to that person in the same way that I'm currently talking to myself?"

I can only speak for myself, but I reserve an exquisite form of shamefulness for myself when I commit a serious mistake. "I'm such an idiot! Why do I always do such stupid things on a daily basis? I need to be banished to a filthy worm-infested hole underneath my house where I can reflect, uninterrupted, on my inescapable stupidity until I prove myself worthy of respect, sunshine, and breathing the same air as my fellow humans."

That's some Thanos-level supervillain type of cruelty right there. I would sooner try to juggle a stack of flaming chainsaws than speak to my two daughters in that way. So, why would I ever consider talking to myself—the guy who is responsible for raising my daughters—in that way? We will make mistakes on this journey, and unfortunately, some of them may deeply harm ourselves or someone else. When that happens, become aware if your feelings of guilt are turning into shame, do whatever is within your power to make it right (and if that's not possible, at least fully own your role in it), and give yourself the self-compassion of speaking to yourself in the same way that you would speak to the person you love the most.

Most of all, please remember this self-compassionate truth that I often tell myself: I am doing the best I can, and if I knew better at the time of my transgression, I would have taken different action.

4. "Is Anything Unforgivable?"

The opinions about what is unforgivable is as wide as the ocean is deep.

I used to work with a woman who said that it was unforgiveable that the caterer she hired for her wedding brought the beef dish instead of the chicken dish for her reception. On the other end of the spectrum, there are people who have forgiven people who killed their loved ones. There are people who have forgiven sexual predators like Larry Nassar. There are people who have forgiven the people who wrongly sent them to prison for crimes they didn't commit (and even forgave the people who falsely testified against them to ensure that it happened). And there are people who have even forgiven the people who were responsible for events in our world's history that are the cause of generational trauma, such as the transatlantic slave trade or the Holocaust. Regardless of the situation, you can think of something that is widely considered a minor transgression and find people who are unable or unwilling to forgive the offender for it. Conversely, you can think of the most diabolical, evil acts that humanity can devise and discover people who will find it in their heart to forgive.

Forgiveness is a choice, and it's a very complex, nuanced, and emotional choice. I have no interest in using this space to tell anyone to do something that they choose not to do, and I'm certainly not qualified to judge what is forgivable or not. I will say this, though—when we are ready to move forward with our lives (however long that takes), forgiveness is what will set us free.

Free from toxic resentment.

Free from being consumed with thoughts of vengeance.

Free from being cruel to ourselves.

Free to reclaim our peace, our happiness, our sanity, and a chance at a good life.

Most of all, free from allowing people who we don't like or respect to live rent-free in our minds anymore.

As Lewis B. Smedes once wisely said, "To forgive is to set a prisoner free and discover that the prisoner was you."

This is the final, and most challenging, bridge we must cross to unite our world behind the power of civility. Instead of focusing on others, this is about choosing to heal ourselves by self-administering the civility that is required for us to survive and, ideally, thrive. We cannot change the past, but we can decide today if we're ready to take a courageous and radical step outside of our self-imposed prison toward healing and a more civil world.

If so, the good news is that we are in possession of the key.

INTENTIONAL CONSISTENT INTERVENTION #26: *FORGIVE OR NOT*

If you feel that completing this ICI would cause additional trauma, please feel free to skip it. You can always return here later, if you choose.

ICI Steps:

1. If you are able and willing, describe the situation where you were harmed in your *Civil Unity Journal*.
2. Ask yourself, "Am I ready to offer forgiveness?" You do not need to forgive anyone; just ask yourself if you are ready. If the answer is "no," that is completely fine.
3. If you are ready to forgive, commit to begin the process today instead of putting it off for a moment longer. Forgiveness is an intensely personal decision—document in your *Civil Unity Journal* what it would mean for you to forgive the person (or people) who hurt you.

CONCLUSION

In every encounter, we either give life or we drain it. There is no neutral exchange.

—BRENNAN MANNING

Sometimes, the moments that change our lives aren't remarkable.

It was December in the 1990s, and I just finished my first semester at Union College in Schenectady, New York. Up to that point, the college experience wasn't anything like the unrealistic expectations that bounced around in my teenage mind. In high school, academics had always come easy for me. I was one of those annoying kids who would study for an exam for the first time on the bus ride to school, and then a few hours later, I would ace the test with ease. Unsurprisingly, that study strategy did not hold up against the rigor of college academics, and for the first time in my life, I was seeing grades of C, D, and F on my transcript.

To make things worse, in high school, I had a large friend group, but I struggled to make friends in college. Most of the freshman students were put into large dormitories in the middle of campus, which meant that they were in the center of all of the action. They were hanging out together after classes in the dorms, enjoying late-night parties, and making lifelong connections. Unfortunately, I drew the short straw and ended up in a small dormitory on the far edge of the campus with eleven other freshmen, which was less than ideal for me—as far as I was concerned, I might as well have been in Siberia. As a young man desperate to fit in, I felt isolated from the fun and friendship aspect of the college experience that was presumably being enjoyed by the other freshmen students. It didn't take long for the constant exclusion to effectively break my heart and my will.

None of this unpleasantness was what I signed up for, and on that December morning, I decided that I was going to quit college. The plan was that I was going to inform my parents about this life-altering decision over the winter break, and then sometime between Christmas and New Year's Day, I would return to campus with a U-Haul truck, pack up my stuff in the middle of the night, and return back to Amherst, Massachusetts, leaving the college experience behind me forever. I still shudder at the utter ridiculousness of this plan, but at the time, I felt like it was a brilliant strategy.

After I finished what I firmly believed was my last college final exam of my life, I packed up my clothes and other essential items that I needed for the winter break, locked my dorm room door, and started walking toward the Greyhound Bus station to catch my ride home. Little did I know what happened next would not only change my life, but it would be largely responsible for this book ending up in your hands.

The Unlikely Encounter

The walk to the bus station from the campus was only a mile, but the difficulty of this trek was dialed up to "ultra-hard mode" because of the weather. If you are not familiar, winters in upstate New York can be brutal, and on this December morning, the weather was some of the worst that I had experienced in my young life. The sidewalks were icy, the wind chill made the air so cold that it was making the hairs in my nostrils crystalize, and of course, because of the wind, it was snowing sideways directly into my face. As much as I tried, I couldn't get a solid footing because of the super slick sidewalks, and I was reduced to shuffling my feet like an uncoordinated penguin while carrying my ridiculously heavy duffel bag on my shoulder. In the 1990s, rolling suitcases were just beginning to become mainstream, and unfortunately, I was behind on that useful trend.

I only had thirty minutes until the last bus before Christmas departed from the bus station to Springfield, Massachusetts, and as I looked down at my watch, it became increasingly unlikely that I would make it. It took me close to an hour to make it halfway to the bus stop, and the weather was only getting worse. Then, to make an already-horrendous situation completely unbearable, the impractically thin shoulder strap broke, and my enormous duffel bag fell with a thud on the icy sidewalk. Carrying a forty-pound bag without a strap in the biting cold and on the slippery ice was going to be an impossibility, and I knew it. At that point, the nightmare that I would be spending my first Christmas away from home being stuck in an empty dorm room in Schenectady was overwhelming. So, I did the only thing that made sense. While standing helplessly on the side of the road, I began to cry.

Within minutes, a car pulled up beside me, and a woman rolled down her driver-side window and allowed the falling snow to pelt her in the face. "Hey, are you going to the bus station?" she asked kindly. I pitifully nodded "yes," and she responded with urgency, "You're never going to make it there in this weather. Hop in, I'll give you a lift." She popped open the trunk of her car for me to throw my bag inside, but I just stood on the sidewalk incredulously as the snow slowly began to fill her open trunk. This was way before Lyft and Uber were on the scene, so jumping into strangers' cars wasn't really a thing that most people at that time were cool with.

"Come on, you must be freezing!" she implored.

Despite my initial reservations, getting warm and *getting home* was too sweet of an offer to refuse. I wiped the tears from my face, dragged my duffel bag through the icy slush toward her car, and mercifully plopped it in her trunk. As I sat in the passenger seat, I thanked her profusely for the ride. She smiled warmly and said, "It's my pleasure to help."

On the short ride to the bus station, she noticed the tears streaked on my face and asked me if I was OK. I shared that I was struggling academically, I didn't have any friends, I was severely homesick, and I was about to drop out of school. The tears began to flow again. She listened without interrupting before offering a piece of kind advice. "You know, the first year of college away from home is always tough. My suggestion, if you're willing, is to be open to the idea that there might be another option besides dropping out. You have a long ride from here to the Springfield bus station. Challenge yourself to see if there's another way, I think you'll be glad that you did." It was clear to me that she spoke from a place of lived experience.

And with that, we arrived at the bus station with fifteen minutes to spare. I wanted to hug her for extending me such extraordinary kindness, but I didn't want to do anything to make her uncomfortable and ruin our wonderful interaction. She patted me on the shoulder and said, "Good luck," as she popped open her trunk for me to retrieve my broken bag. I jumped out of her warm car and back into the cold of the Schenectady winter to grab my things and walk inside of the bus station. As I looked behind me, she waved at me through her closed driver-side window and slowly drove away.

As I sat alone on the bus ride home, I was consumed with unanswered questions. How did she know that I was going to the bus station? What did she mean that "there might be another option besides dropping out of school?" Most of all, what in the world made her stop in the middle of a raging snowstorm to pick up a stranger off the street and offer him a ride? That type of kindness was so foreign to me, and for days afterward, I questioned if that interaction happened or if I made it up.

Because our interaction was so unlikely, I decided to explore the equally unlikely idea that there was another option besides dropping out of school, like she suggested. Upon reflection, I realized that I really didn't put in any effort to make my college experience one that I would enjoy. The sad reality was that I didn't work hard in my classes, I didn't try to make friends, and more empowering, I realized that I had everything within me to make my college experience one that I would enjoy. Upon arriving at Springfield bus station, I decided that was exactly what I was going to do.

My parents never knew that I briefly considered dropping out of school, but I did inform them that I'd likely be on academic probation. Based on their reaction to the probation news, they probably would have both clutched their chests like Redd Foxx from *Sanford and Son* if I stuck with my original plan of telling them that I was going to drop out of school. I pledged to my parents, and to myself, that

I would recommit to my college experience, and that's exactly what happened. Upon returning to campus after winter break, I thrived. It was at Union College where I discovered a love for psychology, a passion for writing, and where I demonstrated for the first time that I was capable of doing hard things—all of which serve as the unshakable foundation of my career today.

I honestly don't know if any of that would have been possible if I dropped out of college, and I don't know if I would have stayed in college if it weren't for the uncommon kindness of a stranger in the middle of a snowstorm.

Give Life or Drain It

It is difficult to overstate how much that interaction affected me.

It happened over thirty years ago, and I doubt that the angelic woman who saved me from the cold on that winter day gave our brief car ride a second thought after she dropped me off. Our ride together to the bus station was short, and in those fifteen minutes together, my life was changed forever. But then again, the same could be said for the sexual abuse that I endured as a child, which lasted approximately the same time. In addition, my suicide attempt was less than a minute. All of these events remain burned into my consciousness decades later, which is a sobering reminder that brief encounters can endure for an astonishingly long time in our hearts and minds.

Brennan Manning's quote at the beginning of this conclusion hits me in my soul every time I read it: "In every encounter, we are either giving life or we are draining it. There is no neutral exchange."

No neutral exchange.

Can you imagine if we lived our lives with that level of fierce intentionality and awareness? Can you picture a world where we embrace our repeated opportunities on a daily basis to give life to others or drain it? Yes, there will always be big moments, but our lives also are full of brief encounters—hundreds of thousands, maybe millions of them in a lifetime. Given those numbers, it is almost guaranteed that there is at least one person walking the earth whose life you have changed forever in a single short-lived encounter. That encounter may be something that you have long forgotten, but they will remember your role in it until the day they die. That is a humbling reality.

So, in that seminal moment—the one encounter where you will be remembered by that person forever—there's only one question that matters: Did you use your time together to give them life, or did you drain it from them? The person on the receiving end of your words, actions, or behaviors knows the answer to that question—but do you?

What makes this even more challenging is that we don't get to choose which seemingly innocuous encounter will be the one that changes someone's life. Our child tugs on our pant leg for our attention while we're busy answering mindless work emails. We are under-caffeinated, running late for work, and the barista who is battling clinical depression just incorrectly prepared our coffee order. Someone directs a bigoted comment toward another person in front of us while we sit in silence. A classmate vulnerably shows you their artwork for the first time. We find a person passed out alone on the couch at a party after drinking too much. A neighbor tells you that they have been thinking that life isn't worth living anymore. The decision points we will face in this lifetime are infinite, but the options will always remain binary: give life or drain it. That's it.

Healing What Is Broken

This book was written in hopes of awakening us to the idea that at our daily decision points, we can always make a radical choice that unites our world and makes it a better place for all of us. I believe that civility is that radical choice. The act of demonstrating respect toward our fellow human beings has a healing effect and an impact that can outlive our years, whether we are aware of it or not. I'm not suggesting that you drive around your town offering free rides to strangers. But, if we are being honest, there is likely an opportunity to give others a gift that will always be appreciated: the acknowledgment of their humanity and a demonstration of respect.

Yes, we will encounter mean-spirited, hateful, and dangerous people who are unworthy of our time and respect, and it will serve us well to distinguish them from everyone else. My argument is that those people are a much smaller percentage of the population than commonly believed. The much larger percentage of humanity may include people who do not look like us, pray like us, vote like us, or think like us on issues that matter to us. Our encounters with them are guaranteed, and since despising them and cursing their existence haven't worked too well, shouldn't we try something else?

Please don't fall for the foolishness that civility means that we shouldn't fight for our beliefs (although it's worth examining why we believe in them so ardently), concede on ideas that may harm us, or refuse to hold people accountable for their actions. Disagreement is necessary in order to have a functioning society; we just need to engage in the work of doing it more effectively.

In our deeply divided world, it is a radical act to refrain from unproductive disrespect toward people who don't see the world as we do. The stakes have never been higher to actively participate in a conscious shift to stop humanity from hating one another, fighting one another, and eventually killing one another. Just like a journey of a thousand miles begins with a single step, the journey to heal our world begins with a single decision in every encounter: give life or drain it.

I have been broken by this world, and maybe you have too. There are times in my most private moments where I am haunted by the cruelty I have experienced and equally overwhelmed by the harshness and brutality in the world around me.

I have also been healed by this world. When my faith in the goodness of humanity is in shambles, I return back to the countless times where I have received warmth, kindness, respect, and civility from strangers in my lifetime. But, in particular, I always return to the woman who picked up a sobbing teenager off the street and gave him a ride to the bus stop in the middle of a snowstorm. What did she tap into in order to make the decision to stop and help me?

Did she know that a random—and very uncommon—act of kindness could inspire a person to spread similar kindness to others?

Did she relate to my pain and sadness and make the courageous choice to do whatever was within her power to alleviate it?

Despite our differences, did she realize that honoring our shared humanity was the only thing that mattered in that moment?

Did she acknowledge that when presented with the choice to either give me life or drain it from me, she chose the only option that would create a more civil world?

I'm not sure, but I promise that I will spend the rest of my life trying to figure it out.

I hope you will join me in that pursuit.

ACKNOWLEDGMENTS

Recently on LinkedIn, one of my contacts, who was writing her first book, asked me, "Since you're on your third book, does the process get any easier?" I can't speak for other authors, but I can confidently say that the answer for me is "no." Sure, I've learned some things along the way like outlining my content, organizing my research, and scheduling dedicated time to write—all of which have been helpful. But the process of overcoming my impostor syndrome, quieting my inner self-talk ("who are you to write about this stuff, Shola?"), staring at the blinking cursor that's taunting me to try to type something meaningful, and pushing past my comfort zone to share deeply personal information has not any gotten easier, and if I choose to do this again, I doubt it ever will.

The only reason why I was able to move forward and keep writing this book is because of the people mentioned next.

First, to my fabulous wife, Amber—there is so much I could say, but I'll simply say this: *Thank you.* Thank you for always having my back. Thank you for creating the space for me to write this book (which, often, was at a great sacrifice for you). Thank you for your unceasing love, support, and friendship. And thank you for not punching me in the face when I said, "So … um, I'm thinking about writing another book." It's often said that the most important decision we'll make in our lives is who we choose as our life partner. In a lifetime of questionable decisions, I can proudly say that I nailed the most crucial one. I love you, babe.

To my daughters, Kaya and Nia—the world is more divided than ever, and I'm confident that both of you will lead the way in bringing us back together. Your kindness, your intelligence (emotional and intellectual), your humor, and your perseverance will serve you both well as you continue to heal the world with your actions and your words. Even though you are fifteen and thirteen years old, respectively, I'm grateful that you both have embraced the reality that you have everything within you now to lead the way. I love you both so much, and always remember that you belong in any room that you walk into.

To my mom—I know that the past five years have been challenging for you with the devastating loss of Dad to cancer. Still though, during this time, you've always found a way to be relentlessly positive, loving, supportive, and incredibly funny. Our phone conversations are the highlight of my day, and my cross-country visits to see you are always the highlights of my year. Despite your own health challenges, thank you so much for your check-ins, positive vibes, and sage advice when I was struggling mightily to write this book. I love you, Mom—Dad would be so proud to see how the love in our family has continued to grow after his passing.

To my brothers, Femi and Doyin—thank you for being there for me and for keeping the mood light in our hilarious "Richards Brothers Group Text." It has been a wild past few years for the three of us, both personally and professionally, but through it all, I am deeply grateful for your love and for the strength of our relationship.

To the team at Gotham Artists—there is no way that I'd ever be in a position to write this book without having you in my corner. Thank you for believing in me and my message and for putting me in front of audiences all over the world where I had the privilege to share my message of civility. In particular, I want to thank Alec Melman, Conner Krizancic, Kate DesRosier, Katie Gonzalez, Liz Cooke, Lizzie Brill, Mike Gottesman, Sam Conine, Sam Vanderhoof, and Theresa Ferron. Y'all are the best—I'm deeply grateful that you took a chance on me when very few people would.

To the fine people at Forbes Books—thank you, not only for publishing *Civil Unity* but also for republishing my first two books, *Making Work Work* and *Go Together*, under the Forbes Books umbrella. A special shout-out to Patti Boysen who advocated tirelessly on my behalf to make it happen. You are both a beast (in the coolest and most awesome usage of the word) and an angel. I appreciate you more than you'll ever know, my friend. In addition, I want to extend huge thanks to David Taylor and Megan Elger for your creative artistry on the covers for all three of my books—I am so grateful that you both kindly chose to give life to my words with your incredible artistic talents. Last, but not least, I want to extend enormous thanks to my editor, Heath Ellison. Specifically, thank you for your patience as I obsessively kept making revision after revision to the submitted manuscript. I may even ask for another revision after I'm done typing this (I'm kidding … I think). Also, thank you for granting me the freedom to write this book in my conversational style, for putting up with my love for parentheses (I really do love them!), and for letting me be my nerdy, vulnerable, and silly self.

To Brian Fields—I can't even put into words how much I appreciate your friendship. Our philosophical discussions, Korean barbeque dinners, long days watching our daughters play club volleyball in musty gyms, and our epic Mario Kart battles will all remain legendary. Most of all, you have been there through the writing of all three of my books with constant encouragement, brilliant insight, kindness, and humor. So grateful for our bond, Broseph.

To my Mastermind Group: Christine Quinn, James Rosseau, and Kris McGuigan. Our time together is always my favorite meeting of the month. Thank you for the space we hold for each other to vulnerably talk about our crushing disappointments, lofty goals, crippling fears, and beautiful successes. Every time that I felt like quitting, the three of you were there to keep me on track and lovingly hold me accountable. Your friendship means the world to me, and I never want to experience a day in my life without it.

To Maria Vega—thank you for your saint-like kindness and for your willingness to offer your extraordinary research skills to this book. When you reached out to me, I was at an impasse in my writing, and your assistance was the spark that allowed me to overcome my writer's block and move forward. I am enormously grateful for you and your expertise.

To my therapist, Eric—more than anyone I've named so far, you are the primary reason why I found the strength to write this book. Your wisdom, patience, thoughtfulness, creativity, humor, and realness helped me to work through some pretty dark stuff. Nothing works without sound mental health, and I'm unquestionably a better father, husband, speaker, writer, and human being because of our sessions together. It's not hyperbole to say that you have changed my life, and one of the best moves that I have ever made in my life was finding you.

And to the people who showed me kindness (and those who didn't)—thank you for serving as the inspiration for this book. Most important, thank you for reinforcing the truth in my heart that the world can be united with kindness and civility and, quite frankly, destroyed without it. My sincerest hope is that this book will be useful in getting others to choose kindness and civility over hate and divisiveness. One thing is for sure, because of you, I know what side of history I'm choosing to be on for the rest of my life.

ABOUT THE AUTHOR

Shola Richards is the CEO and founder of Go Together Global® and the author of *Making Work Work* and *Go Together*, and he is leading a worldwide movement to change the world based on how we treat one another at work, home, and every place in between. Shola's work has been featured on the *Today* show, *CBS This Morning*, *Forbes*, *Black Enterprise*, Complete Wellbeing India, and *Business Insider Australia*, and his tireless efforts to make the world a kinder place have earned him the well-deserved nickname, "Brother Teresa."

As a keynote speaker, Shola has shared his transformative message with Fortune 50 companies, top universities, leading healthcare organizations, Silicon Valley, the motion picture industry, on the TEDx stage, and on three different continents, and in his greatest honor to date, in September 2021, he was invited to testify in front of the House of Representatives on Capitol Hill to share his expert recommendations on how to bring more civility to Congress.

Last, but certainly not least, Shola is a father, husband, identical twin, and a self-professed "kindness extremist" who will not rest until bullying and incivility are extinct from the American workplace. He currently lives in Los Angeles, California, with his wife, two daughters, and his dog, Ace.

You can stay updated with Shola here: www.SholaRichards.com
You can follow Shola on social media here:
Facebook: www.facebook.com/sholarichardsofficial
Instagram/Threads: @sholarichards
LinkedIn: www.linkedin.com/in/sholarichards
Twitter/X: @sholarichards